The *Speedy* Revision Guide

Key Stage 3
Tier 6–8

Speedy Revision

Introduction

 This revision guide is aimed at Tier 6–8 of the KS3 National Tests for Mathematics. It's the perfect size to keep with you at all times during the crucial weeks before the tests.

There is *speedy* coverage of each topic in the four main strands:
- Number
- Algebra
- Shape, space & measures
- Handling data

Everything you need to know about a topic is given on one or two pages, in the same format:
- **Essential facts**
  Everything you need to know, complete with examples.
- **Q & A**
  Easy-to-follow worked examples with clearly explained methods.
- **Check-up TESTs**
  To make sure everything has sunk in. (If you can do all the tests, you are heading in the right direction!)

On pages 74–75 there is a *speedy* revision test to check that you have remembered all the basic facts. (If you're short of time, try the revision test first, then revise those topics you got wrong; that truly is *speedy* revision!)

Good luck in your tests!

Contents

Number

Multiples, factors &
prime factors 4
LCM & HCF 5
Rounding 6
Fractions 8
Percentages 10
Fractions, decimals &
percentages 12
Ratio & proportion 13
Negative numbers 15
Powers & roots 16
Standard index form 18
Calculations with brackets 21

Algebra

Using letters 22
Brackets 23
Equations 24
Formulae & substitution 25
Rearranging formulae 26
Sequences &
number patterns 27
Functions & mappings 29
Straight-line graphs 30
Graphs you should know 32
Real-life graphs 33
Inequalities 34
Simultaneous equations 36
Trial & improvement 38

Shape, space & measures

Units of measurement &
accuracy 39
Angles & parallel lines 40

Polygons 41
Symmetry 42
Transformations 43
Perimeter & circumference 46
Areas of triangles &
quadrilaterals 47
Areas of circles &
composite shapes 48
More circles 49
Pythagoras' theorem 50
Trigonometry 52
Volume & surface area 54
Dimensions 56
Congruent & similar shapes 57
Bearings & scale drawings 59
Compound measures 60
Constructions & loci 61

Handling data

Mean, median, mode, range 63
Discrete & continuous data 64
Collecting data &
two-way tables 65
Frequency tables 66
Stem & leaf diagrams; line
graphs 68
Scatter graphs 69
Cumulative frequency 70
Probability 72

Speedy revision test 74
Answers 76
Index 79

Multiples, factors & prime factors

● Multiples

The multiples of a number are the numbers in its times-table.

> ➤ The multiples of 14 are 14, 28, 42, ...

● Factors

The factors of a number are the numbers that divide into it exactly.

To find all the factors of the number, start at 1 and divide by each whole number in turn. Stop when you get a repeat.

Factors always appear in pairs, i.e. 1 × 15 = 15 and 3 × 5 = 15.

> ➤ **The factors of 15**
>
> 15 ÷ 1 = 15
> 15 ÷ 2 = not a whole number
> 15 ÷ 3 = 5
> 15 ÷ 4 = not a whole number
> 15 ÷ 5 = 3 (Repeats, so stop)
> So the factors of 15 are 1, 3, 5, and 15.

● Prime numbers

A prime number has exactly two factors (itself and 1).

Note: 1 is not a prime number (it has only one factor – itself).

You should memorise the first few primes: 2, 3, 5, 7, 11, 13, 17, ...
Apart from 2, primes are always odd numbers.
Any odd number that's in a times-table other than its own is not a prime number. e.g. 9 is not prime as it's in the 3 times-table.

● Prime factors

Prime numbers that are factors of a number are called prime factors. For example, 3 is a prime factor of 15 (3 is prime and a factor of 15). You can write any number as a product of its prime factors:

> ➤ $20 = 4 \times 5 = 2 \times 2 \times 5 = 2^2 \times 5$
>
> Break 20 into 4 × 5.   Break 4 into 2 × 2.
>
> Only primes left. Rewrite the answer with indices.

---

1 List the first five multiples of these: **a** 5 **b** 8 **c** 6 **d** 9
2 List all the factors of these: **a** 8 **b** 32 **c** 40
3 Write these as products of their prime factors: **a** 36 **b** 84

TEST

LCM & HCF

● Least common multiple

The least common multiple (LCM) is the smallest number that is a multiple of two or more numbers.

To find the LCM of two numbers you could list the multiples of both numbers, then pick out the smallest number that's in both lists. But this can take absolutely ages, so use the prime factorisation method below, it's much quicker.

➤ Q & A

What is the LCM of 15 and 42?

Answer
Prime factorisations are:
$15 = 3 \times 5$
$42 = 2 \times 3 \times 7$
So LCM $= 2 \times 3 \times 5 \times 7 = \underline{210}$

3 appears in both prime factorisations so only include it once.

➤ Method

❶ Write each number as a product of its prime factors.
❷ Combine the prime factorisations counting common factors only once.
❸ Multiply to get the LCM.

● Highest common factor

The highest common factor (HCF) is the largest number that is a factor of two or more numbers.

To find the HCF of two numbers you could list the factors of both numbers, then pick out the largest number that's in both lists. But again this can take absolutely ages, so use the prime factorisation method below, it's again much quicker.

➤ Q & A

What is the HCF of 720 and 84?

Answer
Prime factorisations are:
$720 = 2 \times 2 \times 2 \times 2 \times 3 \times 3 \times 5$
$84 = 2 \times 2 \times 3 \times 7$
So HCF $= 2 \times 2 \times 3 = \underline{12}$

➤ Method

❶ Write each number as a product of its prime factors.
❷ Pick out all the prime factors common to both prime factorisations.
❸ Multiply them together to get the HCF.

---

1 What is the LCM of **a** 16 and 36 **b** 50 and 95?
2 What is the HCF of **a** 36 and 48 **b** 820 and 252?
3 Give the LCM and HCF of 12, 42 and 56.

TEST

Rounding (1)

● Rounding to the nearest ten

❶ <u>Focus</u> on the <u>tens digit</u>.

$$37\underset{\uparrow}{2}1.6 \quad \text{⟶} \quad 3720$$

❷ If the number to the <u>right</u> of the <u>tens digit</u> (i.e. the units) is <u>5 or more, round up</u>. Otherwise the tens digit <u>stays the same</u>.

❸ <u>Get rid of</u> everything to the <u>right</u> of the tens column. Remember to put a <u>zero as a place holder</u> in the units column.

● Rounding to the nearest hundred, thousand, ...

Do this the same way as rounding to the nearest ten, but <u>focus on the hundreds or thousands</u> digit.

> ### ➤ Example
> 3721.6 → 3700 to nearest 100
> 3721.6 → 4000 to nearest 1000

● Rounding to decimal places

'<u>Decimal place</u>' is often abbreviated to '<u>dp</u>' or '<u>d.p.</u>'.

When rounding to <u>1 dp</u> focus on the <u>1st</u> digit after the decimal point. For <u>2 dp</u>, <u>3 dp</u>, ... focus on the <u>2nd</u>, <u>3rd</u>, ... digit after the decimal point.

➤ Q & A

Round 0.168 to 2 dp.

Answer

Focus on the 2nd decimal place.

$$0.1\underset{\nwarrow}{6}8 \quad \text{⟶} \quad 0.17$$

8 is '5 or more', so round 6 <u>up</u> to 7.

➤ Method (rounding to 2 dp)

❶ Focus on the 2nd dp.
❷ If the digit to the <u>right</u> of the 2nd dp is <u>5 or more, round upwards</u>. Otherwise the 2nd dp <u>stays the same</u>.
❸ <u>Get rid</u> of everything to the <u>right</u> of the 2nd dp.

Rounding (2)

● Rounding to significant figures

The 1st significant figure is the 1st non-zero digit from the left.

The 2nd, 3rd, ... significant figures are the digits immediately after the 1st significant figure, even if they are zeros.

'Significant figures' is often shortened to 'sig figs', 'sig. figs.', 'sf' or 's.f.'.

➤ Example

	1st	2nd	3rd	4th

$$0.05096$$

➤ Q & A

Round 5384 to 2 sig figs.

Answer

Focus on the 2nd sig fig.

5384 ⟹ 5400

8 is '5 or more', so round upwards.

Add zeros. (It would be silly to round to 54.)

➤ Method (rounding to 2 sf)

❶ Focus on the 2nd sig fig.

❷ If the digit to the right of the 2nd sig fig is 5 or more, round upwards. Otherwise the 2nd sig fig stays the same.

❸ Get rid of everything to the right of the 2nd sig fig. (Add zeros as place holders if needed.)

● Some extra rounding examples

Make sure you can see how these were rounded.

	to 1 dp	to 2 dp	to 3 dp	to 1 sf	to 2 sf	to 3 sf
24.9374	24.9	24.94	24.937	20	25	24.9
0.9527	1.0	0.95	0.953	1	0.95	0.953
0.07457	0.1	0.07	0.075	0.07	0.075	0.0746
888.8888	888.9	888.89	888.889	900	890	889

1 Round these to the nearest hundred: 27 920, 2875, 62

2 Round these to 2 dp: 0.582, 0.019, 12.882

3 Round these to 2 sf: 352, 1.006, 0.809

4 Estimate the answers to these by first rounding all numbers to 1 sf: **a** $\dfrac{(5.45 + 10.85)}{2.86}$ **b** $\dfrac{(989 \times 304)}{296}$

TEST

Speedy Revision

Fractions (1)

A fraction shows the number of parts out of the whole.

The top is the numerator. → **3**
← 3 parts are shaded ...

The bottom is the denominator. → **5**
← ... out of 5

> **Example**
> $\frac{3}{5}$ is three-fifths.
>
> $\frac{3}{5}$ means 3 out of 5.

● Equivalent fractions

You can find equivalent fractions by multiplying/dividing top and bottom by the same number.

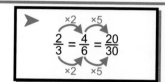

$$\frac{2}{3} = \frac{4}{6} = \frac{20}{30}$$

(×2, ×5 above; ×2, ×5 below)

● Simplifying fractions

To write a fraction in its simplest form divide numerator and denominator (top and bottom) by the highest common factor.

This is often called 'cancelling'.

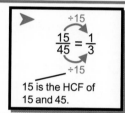

$$\frac{15}{45} = \frac{1}{3}$$ (÷15)

15 is the HCF of 15 and 45.

● Adding/subtracting fractions

You can only add/subtract fractions once they have the same denominator.

$$\frac{2}{3} + \frac{1}{5} = \frac{10}{15} + \frac{3}{15} = \frac{10 + 3}{15} = \frac{13}{15}$$

● Improper & mixed fractions

Improper fractions are 'top heavy', i.e. the numerator is bigger than the denominator.
Mixed numbers are made up of a whole number and a fraction.

> $\frac{8}{5}$ is an improper fraction.
> $3\frac{3}{5}$ is a mixed number.

---

1 Write down the fraction that is shaded: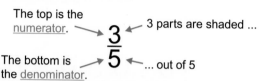

2 Write as a fraction in its simplest form: **a** $\frac{4}{6}$ **b** $\frac{12}{16}$ **c** 4p out of 10p

3 Work out **a** $\frac{2}{9} + \frac{2}{3}$ **b** $\frac{3}{4} - \frac{5}{8}$.

4 Write $1\frac{2}{3}$ as an improper fraction.

5 Write $\frac{10}{3}$ as a mixed number.

TEST

8

Fractions (2)

● Multiplying fractions

You multiply the numerators, then you multiply the denominators.

> **Example**

$$\frac{3}{4} \times \frac{5}{7} = \frac{3 \times 5}{4 \times 7} = \frac{15}{28}$$

Sometimes you can cancel out common factors to make the multiplication easier:

> **Example**

$$\frac{9}{10} \times \frac{15}{36} = \frac{\overset{1}{\cancel{9}}}{10} \times \frac{15}{\underset{4}{\cancel{36}}} = \frac{\overset{1}{\cancel{9}}}{\underset{2}{\cancel{10}}} \times \frac{\overset{3}{\cancel{15}}}{\underset{4}{\cancel{36}}} = \frac{1 \times 3}{2 \times 4} = \frac{3}{8}$$

9 is a common factor of 9 and 36, so you can cancel these out (there is 1 nine in 9 and 4 nines in 36).

5 is a common factor of 10 and 15, so you can cancel these out (there are 2 fives in 10 and 3 fives in 15).

● Dividing fractions

To divide fractions, you turn the second one over and then multiply.

> **Example**

$$\frac{2}{9} \div \frac{3}{7} = \frac{2}{9} \times \frac{7}{3} = \frac{2 \times 7}{9 \times 3} = \frac{14}{27}$$

● Fraction of

To find one-third of something you divide by three.

To find two-thirds, you find a third then multiply by two.

You can find other fractions exactly the same way – find one part then multiply.

> **Example**

$\frac{1}{3}$ of £60 = £60 ÷ 3 = £20

↓ ×2   ↓ ×2

$\frac{2}{3}$ of £60 = £20 × 2 = £40

● Fractions on your calculator

Your calculator should have a button that looks like **a^b/c**.

To work out $\frac{2}{9} \div \frac{3}{7}$ press **2** **a^b/c** **9** **÷** **3** **a^b/c** **7** **=** to get

| 14_27 | in your display. This means the answer is $\frac{14}{27}$.

---

1 a $\frac{5}{7} \times \frac{2}{7}$ **b** $\frac{6}{8} \times \frac{8}{9}$ **c** $\frac{2}{9} \div \frac{2}{3}$ **d** $\frac{4}{7} \div \frac{8}{9}$ **e** Find $\frac{2}{5}$ of £55.

2 Check your answers to **Q1** on a calculator.

TEST

Percentages (1)

Make sure you know how to change percentages to fractions and decimals (p12).

● Percentage of

➤ Q & A

Find 20% of £400.

Answer

$\frac{20}{100}$ × £400 = £80

or 0.2 × £400 = £80

➤ Method

❶ Write the percentage as a fraction or decimal.

❷ Multiply by the amount given.

● Percentage increase/decrease

➤ Q & A

The price of a game is reduced by 20%. If it cost £30 originally, what is the sale price?

Answer

Decrease = 0.2 × £30 = £6

Sale price = £30 − £6 = £24

➤ Method

❶ Find the decrease (or increase).

❷ Take it off the price. (Add it for an increase.)

Note: Decreasing by 20% is the same as multiplying by 1 − 0.2 = 0.8, so you could work out 0.8 × £30 = £24.

● Finding the price before a percentage decrease

Always think of the original price as 100% and work out what percentage the price you're given is. (It will be less than 100%.)

➤ Q & A

In a sale, all items are reduced by 25%. If a coat costs £37.50 in the sale, how much did it cost originally?

Answer Think of the original price as 100%. The cost now is 100% − 25% = 75%.

0.75 × original price = £37.50

So original price = £37.50 ÷ 0.75 = £50

➤ Method

❶ Work out what percentage the price is now.

❷ Write this as a multiplication.

❸ Divide to find the original price.

Speedy Revision

Percentages (2)

● Finding the price before a percentage increase

You use the <u>same method</u>, but the price now is more than 100%.

➤ Q & A

A new set of golf clubs cost £470 including VAT. What was the price before VAT was added?

Answer

Think of the price <u>before</u> VAT as 100%.
Price <u>including</u> VAT is 100% + 17.5%
= 117.5% = 1.175.

1.175 × original price = £470

So original price = £470 ÷ 1.175 = <u>£400</u>

➤ Method

❶ Work out <u>what percentage</u> the price is <u>now</u>.
❷ Write this as a <u>multiplication</u>.
❸ <u>Divide</u> to find the <u>original price</u>.

● Percentage change

Learn this formula.

$$\text{Percentage change} = \frac{\text{Actual change}}{\text{Original quantity}} \times 100\%$$

➤ Q & A

Dave bought a football for £32.
He then sold it for £36.
What was the percentage increase in price?

➤ Method

❶ Work out the <u>actual change</u>.
❷ Write the <u>original quantity</u>.
❸ Use the <u>formula</u> to work out the <u>percentage change</u>.

Answer

Actual change = £36 − £32 = £4   Original price = £32

So percentage change = $\frac{4}{32}$ × 100% = <u>12.5% increase</u>

With money, percentage change is called percentage profit or loss; this was a <u>12.5% profit</u>.

---

1 **a** What is 15% of 250 g?   **b** Decrease 250 g by 15%.
2 A jumper is reduced by 10% to £18.
   What was the price before the reduction?
3 The cost including VAT is £94. Take off the VAT (at 17.5%).
4 Lauren bought an electronic keyboard for £112, then sold it for £98. What was the percentage loss?

TEST

Fractions, decimals & percentages (1)

● Equivalents you should know

$\frac{1}{2} = 0.5 = 50\%$ $\frac{1}{10} = 0.1 = 10\%$ $\frac{1}{3} = 0.333... = 33\frac{1}{3}\%$

$\frac{1}{4} = 0.25 = 25\%$ $\frac{1}{100} = 0.01 = 1\%$ $\frac{2}{3} = 0.666... = 66\frac{2}{3}\%$

$\frac{3}{4} = 0.75 = 75\%$ $\frac{1}{8} = 0.125 = 12.5\%$

● Converting fractions to decimals

Divide the numerator by the denominator (use a written method or a calculator to do the division).

➤ **Example**
$\frac{2}{5} = 2 \div 5 = 0.4$

● Converting percentages to fractions

Write the percentage as a fraction with denominator 100.

➤ $40\% = \frac{40}{100} = \frac{2}{5}$ Simplify if you can.

● Converting fractions to percentages

Write the fraction as an equivalent fraction with denominator 100.

Then write the numerator with a % sign.

➤ **Example**
$\frac{1}{5} = \frac{20}{100} = 20\%$

● Converting percentages to decimals

This is pretty simple, just divide by 100. Remember to get rid of the % symbol.

➤ **Example**
$15\% = 15 \div 100 = 0.15$

● Converting decimals to fractions

If there is one decimal place, write it over 10.

If there are two decimal places, write them over 100.

➤ **Examples**
$0.8 = \frac{8}{10} = \frac{4}{5}$
$0.12 = \frac{12}{100} = \frac{3}{25}$

Simplify fractions when possible.

1 Convert to fractions: **a** 11% **b** 5% **c** 0.6 **d** 0.15
2 Convert $\frac{7}{10}$ to **a** a decimal **b** a percentage.
3 Convert 0.35 to a fraction.

TEST

Speedy Revision

Fractions, decimals & percentages (2)

● Ordering fractions, decimals & percentages

➤ Q & A

Order this list, smallest first.

1.3, 115%, 225%, $1\frac{1}{3}$

Answer

1.30, 1.15, 2.25, 1.33...

1.30, 1.15, 1.33..., 2.25

1.15, 1.30, 1.33..., 2.25

115%, 1.3, $1\frac{1}{3}$, 225%

➤ Method

❶ Convert any fractions or percentages to decimals.

❷ Compare whole numbers. Order the list by these.

❸ If several have the same whole number, order these by tenths.

❹ Repeat for hundredths, thousandths and so on.

❺ Rewrite the list with the original fractions & percentages in place.

Write these in order, smallest first: 4.2, 145%, 3.45, $4\frac{1}{8}$

Ratio & proportion (1)

● Proportion

'What proportion?' just means
'What fraction?',
'What percentage?' or
'What decimal?'

➤ Example

1 in every 4 squares is shaded.

The proportion shaded is $\frac{1}{4}$ or 25% or 0.25.

● Ratio

In the example, 1 in every 4 squares is red.

So there is 1 red square for every 3 white squares.

The ratio of red to white squares is 1 : 3.   ▮ : ▯▯▯

● Simplifying ratios

Ratios can be simplified like fractions.
Divide both sides by the same number.
If you can't divide any more you have the simplest form.

➤
÷50
50 : 100 = 1 : 2
÷50
1 : 2 is the simplest form.

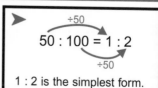

Ratio & proportion (2)

➤ Q & A

It is 1.75 km to the shop and 2500 m to the library.

What is the ratio of the distances?

Answer

1.75 : 2.5   [in km]

175 : 250   [×100]

7 : 10   [÷25]

➤ Method

❶ Write the amounts in the same units.

❷ Write the two amounts without units as 'amount 1 : amount 2'.

❸ If necessary, multiply both sides by any big number to get rid of decimals/fractions.

❹ Divide by the HCF to simplify.

● Dividing in a given ratio

➤ Q & A

Divide £120 in the ratio 2 : 3.

Answer

2 + 3 = 5 parts

1 part is £120 ÷ 5 = £24

2 parts are £24 × 2 = £48

3 parts are £24 × 3 = £72

£48 : £72

➤ Method

❶ Add the ratio to find the total number of parts.

❷ Find the value of 1 part.

❸ Multiply by the number of parts on each side of the ratio.

● Solving problems

➤ Q & A

5 apples cost 90p.

How much would 8 apples cost?

Answer

5 apples cost:	90p
1 apple costs:	90p ÷ 5 = 18p
8 apples cost:	18p × 8 = 144p or £1.44

➤ Method

❶ Divide by 5 to find the cost of 1.

❷ Multiply by 8 to find the cost of 8.

---

1 Simplify: **a** 3 : 18   **b** 27 : 15   **c** 14 km : 120 m

2 Divide 800 ml in the ratio 3 : 7.

3 8 notebooks cost £3.60. How much will 15 cost?

TEST

Negative numbers

● Adding and subtracting

Use a number line to help you add or subtract negative numbers.

➤ **Q & A** What is 3 – 7?

Answer

Start at 3 and count back 7 places, giving an answer of –4.

➤ **Q & A** What is –3 – (–8)?

Answer

First of all deal with the 'minus minus'; together they make a plus.

So –3 – (–8) = –3 + 8

Start at –3 and count forward 8 places, giving an answer of 5.

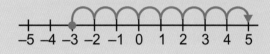

● Multiplying and dividing

Remember these rules for multiplying or dividing negative numbers.

❶ If the signs are the same, the answer is positive (+ + or – – is +).

❷ If the signs are different, the answer is negative (+ – or – + is –).

➤ **Examples**

The signs are the same:	+6 × +2 = +12	+6 ÷ +2 = +3
	–6 × –2 = +12	–6 ÷ –2 = +3
The signs are different:	–6 × +2 = –12	–6 ÷ +2 = –3
	+6 × –2 = –12	+6 ÷ –2 = –3

● The sign change button

Your calculator will have a button like one of these: **+/–** **(–)**.
Make sure you know how to enter negative numbers with it.

Work these out and then check your answers using a calculator.

a 24 ÷ –6   b –5 × –6   c –12 × 12

d 3 – 6   e –14 – 12   f –34 – (–54)

TEST

Powers & roots (1)

● Powers

Powers are just a short way of writing repeated multiplication.

The '<u>power</u>' or '<u>index</u>' tells you how many times the number appears in the repeated multiplication.

> **➤ Example**
> $5^4 = 5 \times 5 \times 5 \times 5 = 625$
>
> The <u>power is 4</u>, so 5 appears <u>4 times</u>.
>
> 5^4 is '5 to the power of 4'.

● Special powers

Any non-zero number '<u>to the power of 0</u>' is 1.
Any number '<u>to the power of 1</u>' is itself.

> **➤ Examples**
> $1^0 = 1$, $2^0 = 1$, $9^0 = 1$
> $1^1 = 1$, $2^1 = 2$, $5^1 = 5$

● Square and cube roots

<u>Finding the root</u> is the opposite (or inverse) of <u>finding the power</u>.

'What is the <u>square root of 16</u>?' means the same as 'What number <u>squared is 16</u>?'

> **➤ Example**
> $\sqrt{16} = 4$ or -4
> as $4 \times 4 = 16$
> and $-4 \times -4 = 16$

➤ Q & A

What is $\sqrt[3]{125}$?

Answer

This is the short way of writing 'What number is the cube root of 125?'

So ask yourself 'What number cubed is 125?'

The answer to this is 5:

$5 \times 5 \times 5 = 125$, so $\sqrt[3]{125} = \underline{5}$

➤ Method

❶ Check whether you are taking the <u>square or cube root</u>.
❷ Ask yourself <u>what number squared/cubed</u> gives the number in the question.
❸ Remember that <u>square roots</u> can be <u>negative</u>.

● Negative powers

A <u>negative power</u> is the <u>reciprocal</u> of a <u>positive power</u>.

('Reciprocal' just means '<u>one over</u>'.)

> **➤ Examples**
> $10^{-3} = \frac{1}{10^3} = \frac{1}{1000} = 0.001$
> $6^{-1} = \frac{1}{6^1} = \frac{1}{6}$

Powers & roots (2)

● Working with powers

◆ To <u>multiply powers</u> of the same number <u>add the indices</u>.

◆ To <u>divide powers</u> of the same number <u>subtract the indices</u>.

◆ To take the <u>power of a power</u> <u>multiply the indices</u>.

> **Examples**
>
> $4^2 \times 4^3 = 4^{2+3} = 4^5$
>
> $3^7 \div 3^4 = 3^{7-4} = 3^3$
>
> $(10^2)^6 = 10^{2 \times 6} = 10^{12}$

> **Q & A** What is $12^9 \div 12^7$?
>
> Answer
>
> $12^9 \div 12^7 = 12^{9-7} = 12^2 = \underline{144}$

> **Method**
>
> ❶ Use the <u>above rules</u> to <u>simplify</u> the calculation.
>
> ❷ <u>Evaluate</u> the power.

● Fractional powers

These are just another way of showing roots. The <u>denominator</u> (bottom) of the fraction <u>tells you which root</u> to take.

> $25^{\frac{1}{2}} = \sqrt{25} = 5$
>
> $8^{\frac{1}{3}} = \sqrt[3]{8} = 2$

● Powers & roots on your calculator

You should have some buttons like these on your calculator:

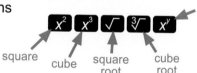

'power' button

square   cube   square root   cube root

To work out $\sqrt{169}$, press **√** **1** **6** **9** **=**. On some calculators you press **√** after you enter the number, i.e. **1** **6** **9** **√**. Sometimes **√** is a '2nd function' written above **x^2**. If your calculator is like this you have to press **SHIFT** **x^2** **1** **6** **9** **=**. To work out 5^8, press **5** **x^y** **8** **=**.

---

1 Find these powers: **a** 12^2 **b** 4^3 **c** 2^5 **d** 8^0 **e** 100^1 **f** 10^{-2}

2 Find these roots: **a** $\sqrt{36}$ **b** $\sqrt{64}$ **c** $\sqrt[3]{1000}$ **d** $27^{\frac{1}{3}}$

3 Combine these powers: **a** $7^4 \times 7^3$ **b** $2^{10} \div 2^5$ **c** $(5^8)^3$

Check your answers to questions **1** and **2** on your calculator.

TEST

Standard index form (1)

● Writing numbers in standard index form

Standard index form (sometimes just called standard form) is a short way of writing really small or large numbers.

A number written in standard form is always 'something times 10 to the power of something':

The first number is always a number between 1 and 10. (It can be 1 but not 10.)

The power of 10 tells you how far the decimal point has moved.

$$3 \times 10^9$$

Written the long way, this number is 3 000 000 000.

➤ Q & A

Write 36 000 in standard form.

Answer

The decimal point needs to move 4 places to get to a number between 1 and 10: 3.6000

36 000 is greater than 1, so the power of 10 is positive.

So, in standard form, the number is written as 3.6×10^4.

➤ Method

❶ Move the decimal point until the number is between 1 and 10.

❷ The power of 10 is the number of places the decimal point moved.

❸ If the original number was greater than 1 then the power is positive.

❹ If the original number was smaller than 1 then the power is negative.

➤ Q & A

Write 0.0045 in standard form.

Answer

The decimal point needs to move 3 places to get to a number between 1 and 10: $0.004.5$

0.0045 is less than 1, so the power of 10 is negative.

So, in standard form, the number is written as 4.5×10^{-3}.

Write these numbers in standard index form:

a 345   b 0.000 24   c 45 000

d 764 000 000   e 0.000 002 453   f 10 million

TEST

Standard index form (2)

● Changing back to normal numbers

➤ Q & A
Write 2.3×10^{-5} as a normal number.

Answer
The power of 10 is <u>negative</u> so we are dealing with a number less than 1, and the decimal point needs to move 5 places to the <u>left</u>:

Put extra zeros in ➤ $0.00002.3$

So the answer is <u>0.000 023</u>.

➤ Method
Move the decimal point the <u>number of places</u> indicated by the <u>power</u> of 10.

Remember, a <u>negative power</u> means that the number is <u>less than 1</u>.

● Multiplying or dividing

➤ Q & A
Work out $(6 \times 10^5) \times (2 \times 10^4)$.

Answer
$(6 \times 10^5) \times (2 \times 10^4)$
$= (6 \times 2) \times (10^5 \times 10^4)$
$= 12 \times 10^{5+4}$
$= 12 \times 10^9$
$= \underline{1.2 \times 10^{10}}$

➤ Q & A
Work out $(8 \times 10^7) \div (2 \times 10^3)$.

Answer
$(8 \times 10^7) \div (2 \times 10^3)$
$= (8 \div 2) \times (10^7 \div 10^3)$
$= 4 \times 10^{7-3}$
$= \underline{4 \times 10^4}$

➤ Method
❶ Rewrite with the '<u>numbers between 1 and 10</u>' at the <u>front</u> and the '<u>powers of 10</u>' together at the <u>end</u>.
❷ <u>Multiply/divide</u> the numbers in the new groups.
❸ Give the <u>answer</u> in <u>standard form</u> (unless asked not to).

See page 17 if you don't know how to multiply or divide powers.

Write these as normal numbers:
a 3.7×10^3 **b** 4.4×10^{-4} **c** 5.43×10^6 **d** 1.2×10^{-6}

TEST

Standard index form (3)

● Adding or subtracting

➤ Q & A
Work out $(2.5 \times 10^5) + (3.4 \times 10^4)$.

Answer
$(2.5 \times 10^5) + (3.4 \times 10^4)$
$= 250\ 000 + 34\ 000$
$= 284\ 000$
$= \underline{2.84 \times 10^5}$

➤ **Method**
❶ Change the numbers to normal numbers.
❷ Add or subtract the numbers.
❸ Give the answer in standard form (unless asked not to).

● Standard index form with a calculator

Your calculator will have a button that looks like one of these:
EXP **E** **EE** **×10ˣ**. This is the standard form button.

To enter a standard form number like 4.6×10^{11} into your calculator just press **4** **●** **6** **EXP** **1** **1** **=** and you'll get something like `4.6 ¹¹` on your display.

➤ Q & A
Use your calculator to work out $(4 \times 10^9) + (5 \times 10^{10})$.

Answer

Press **4** **EXP** **9** **+** **5** **EXP** **1** **0** **=**

and you'll get `5.4 ¹⁰`. This means the answer is $\underline{5.4 \times 10^{10}}$.

(Do not write 5.4^{10}, that means something else!)

---

1 Give your answers to these in standard index form.

   a $(5 \times 10^5) \times (4 \times 10^4)$ **b** $(4.1 \times 10^3) \times (2 \times 10^4)$

   c $(8 \times 10^9) \div (4 \times 10^6)$ **d** $(1.4 \times 10^{-2}) \div (7 \times 10^{-4})$

   e $(2 \times 10^5) + (4 \times 10^4)$ **f** $(6.4 \times 10^3) + (7 \times 10^4)$

   g $(8 \times 10^{-3}) - (4 \times 10^{-3})$ **h** $(8.2 \times 10^7) - (7 \times 10^5)$

2 Check your answers to **Q1** on your calculator.

TEST

Speedy Revision

Calculations with brackets

● Order of operations

When faced with something like $5^2 - 2 \times (7 - 3)$ you have to work out each part in the correct order, else you'll get the wrong answer. Always do operations in this order:

Brackets $\quad\quad\quad\quad\quad 5^2 - 2 \times (7 - 3)$
Squares $\quad\quad\quad\quad\ = 5^2 - 2 \times 4$
Divide and Multiply $= 25 - 2 \times 4$
Add and Subtract $\ \ = 25 - 8$
$\quad\quad\quad\quad\quad\quad\quad = 17$

- -

You can remember the order of operations with the word **BIDMAS**. **B**rackets, then **I**ndices, **D**ivision, **M**ultiplication, **A**ddition, **S**ubtraction. ('Indices' is the fancy word for squares, cubes, etc.)

- -

If there are several multiplications and divisions (or additions and subtractions) do them one at a time from left to right.

For example: Not:

$24 \div 6 \div 2$ $24 \div 6 \div 2$

$= 4 \div 2$ $= 24 \div 3$

$= 2$ ✔ $= 8$ ✘

● Brackets on a calculator

Use the bracket buttons, **( )** , on your calculator exactly where they appear in a calculation. For $72 - (18 + 36)$ press:

7 2 − (1 8 + 3 6) = to get 18.

Look out for sneaky brackets:

$\dfrac{16 - 10}{2}$ is really $(16 - 10) \div 2$, so you have to use brackets.

Press: **(1 6 − 1 0) ÷ 2 =** ✔

Not: **1 6 − 1 0 ÷ 2 =** ✘

Work these out on paper. Check your answers on a calculator.

a $3 \times 5 - 2 \times 4$ **b** $2.8 \times (15 - 2)$ **c** $56 \div 4 \div 2$ **d** $\dfrac{28}{(11 + 3)}$

TEST

Using letters

In algebra, letters represent <u>unknown numbers</u> or numbers that can <u>change</u>.

$n - 1$ means <u>one less</u> than n

$n + 5$ means <u>five more</u> than n

$n + n$ means <u>two lots of n</u> or $2 \times n$

> ➤ **Example**
> Think of a number. I don't know what number you are thinking of, so I'll call it n.

● Terms and expressions

A <u>term</u> is some numbers and letters multiplied together.

$$4a + b + 3ab + 2$$

a term b term ab term   number term

A collection of terms like this is called an <u>expression</u>.

● Collecting like terms

$4a$ and $3a$ are <u>like terms</u> because they have the <u>same letters</u>.

$2a$ and $5b$ are <u>not like terms</u> because they have <u>different letters</u>.

You can <u>simplify</u> expressions by <u>collecting like terms</u>.

$$4a \quad + \quad 3a \quad = \quad 7a$$

'<u>4</u> lots of a' and '<u>3</u> lots of a' makes '<u>7</u> lots of a'.

● Algebraic fractions

Algebraic fractions are fractions with letters in such as $\frac{x}{5}$ or $\frac{2x + 3}{3}$. They may look odd, but you just treat them as normal fractions.

➤ **Q & A**

Work out $\frac{x}{3} + \frac{4x}{3}$.

Answer

The denominators are the same, so it's just a case of adding the numerators: $\frac{x}{3} + \frac{4x}{3} = \frac{x + 4x}{3} = \frac{5x}{3}$

---

1 Simplify these expressions by collecting like terms:

   a $t + t + t$ **b** $n + n + n + n$ **c** $y + 2y$ **d** $3x + 2 + x$

2 Add these fractions: **a** $\frac{2x}{5} + \frac{4x}{5}$ **b** $\frac{1}{d} + \frac{2}{d}$

TEST

Speedy **Revision**

Brackets

● Multiplying out single brackets

To get rid of brackets from an expression, you have to multiply everything inside the brackets by the term outside.
This is also called 'expanding brackets'.

> The 3 multiplies the x and the 2.
>
> $$3(x + 2) = 3 \times x + 3 \times 2 = 3x + 6$$
>
> Outside   Inside
>
> $3(m - 4) = 3m - 12$ $x(y + z) = xy + xz$ $a(4a + b) = 4a^2 + ab$

If the term outside the brackets is negative, you have to change the sign of each term inside the brackets when you multiply out.

> $$-2(a + 3) = -2a - 6$$ $$-3(c - d) = -3c + 3d$$
>
> A plus becomes a minus.   A minus becomes a plus.

● Multiplying out double brackets

➤ Q & A

Simplify $(a + 3)(a - 2)$.

Answer   *Beak* It doesn't need to be a work of art – just join each term in the first bracket to each term in the second.

$(a + 3)(a - 2)$

$= (a \times a) + (a \times -2) + (3 \times a) + (3 \times -2)$
Left eyebrow   Mouth   Nose   Right eyebrow

$= a^2 - 2a + 3a - 6$

$= a^2 + a - 6$

➤ Method

❶ Draw a face with two eyebrows, a nose and a mouth:

❷ Multiply together the terms that are joined by lines.

❸ Collect like terms together.

Multiply out these brackets:
a $4(x + 2)$ **b** $m(n + 7)$ **c** $a(a + b)$ **d** $-4(d - 5)$
e $(x + 2)(x + 3)$ **f** $(x + 2)(x - 5)$ **g** $(x + 1)^2$

TEST

Equations

● Equations

An <u>equation</u> shows that two expressions are <u>equal</u>, e.g. $2x + 4 = 3x$.

● Solving equations

Solving equations is about finding the <u>value of the unknown</u> letter. You can <u>add</u>, <u>subtract</u>, <u>multiply</u> or <u>divide</u> both sides by the same number, but you must do <u>exactly the same</u> thing <u>to both sides</u>.

➤ Q & A

Solve $7x - 4 = 10$ to find the value of x.

Answer

You need to end up with $x = $ something.

Get rid of the − 4 by adding 4 to both sides.

$$7x - 4 = 10$$
$$7x - 4 + 4 = 10 + 4 \qquad \text{[+4 to \underline{both} sides]}$$
$$7x = 14$$
$$7x \div 7 = 14 \div 7 \qquad \text{[÷ \underline{both} sides by 7]}$$
$$\underline{x = 2}$$

Get rid of the × 7 by dividing both sides by 7 ($7x$ means $x \times 7$).

● Two important examples

There are two further types of equations they could throw at you:

❶ <u>The equation contains brackets</u>, e.g. $2(x + 5) = 18$
The first thing to do is to <u>multiply out the brackets</u> (see previous page). Here, the equation becomes $2x + 10 = 18$.
You then solve it as normal (like above **Q & A**, but −10 then ÷2).

❷ <u>The unknown letter appears on both sides</u>, e.g. $5x = 2x + 6$
You need to get the <u>letters</u> on <u>one side</u> and <u>numbers</u> on the <u>other</u>. In this case, subtract $2x$ from both sides to get $3x = 6$.
You then solve it as normal (try dividing both sides by 3 ...)

---

1 Solve these equations: **a** $2x + 5 = 11$ **b** $3x - 8 = 16$
2 Finish solving the 'Two important examples', then solve:
   a $4(2x + 3) = 28$ **b** $10x = 3x + 14$

TEST

Speedy Revision

Formulae & substitution

● Formulae

A <u>formula</u> is basically a rule that <u>turns one number into another</u>.

> ### ➤ Example
>
> Jo has a machine that makes chocolate biscuits.
> One packet of biscuit mix makes four biscuits.
>
> You can write this as a formula in words:
>
> <u>Number of biscuits = 4 × the number of packets of biscuit mix</u>
>
> You can also write this with algebra as <u>$B = 4P$</u>,
> where <u>B</u> represents <u>the number of biscuits</u> and <u>P</u> represents
> <u>the number of packets of biscuit mix</u>.

● Substituting numbers into formulae & expressions

You can <u>substitute</u> a number into an <u>expression</u> to find its value.

To substitute $y = 3$ into $2y + 5$, just write '3' in place of 'y' then work out the answer.

> ➤ When $y = 3$:
> $$2y + 5$$
> $$= 2 \times 3 + 5$$
> $$= 6 + 5$$
> $$= 11$$

The trickiest substitution they could give you is one involving squares or cubes:

➤ Q & A

Given the formula $y = 4x^3$, find the value of y when $x = 2$.

Answer

Write out the formula again with 2 in the place of x:

$y = 4 \times 2^3$ ← 2^3 means 2 times by itself 3 times

$= 4 \times 2 \times 2 \times 2$

$= \underline{32}$ ← Double 4, then double again, then double again!

TEST

1   A plumber charges £25 per hour. Write a formula, in algebra, for the charge (C) in terms of number of hours worked (h).
2   Use your formula from **Q1** to work out the charge for 8 hours.
3   Work out the value of a when $b = 3$ in these formulae:
    a $a = 3b + 2$ **b** $a = 2b^2 + 1$

Rearranging formulae

Making x the subject of a formula means rewriting it as $x = ...$
The formula often has a power of the subject or the subject occurs twice.

● What to do with powers of the subject

➤ Q & A

Make x the subject of $y = 36x^2$.

Answer

$y = 36x^2$

$\sqrt{y} = 6x$ [square root]

$\dfrac{\sqrt{y}}{6} = x$ [÷6]

$x = \dfrac{\sqrt{y}}{6}$ [rewrite]

➤ Method
❶ If the subject has been squared, square root both sides of the equation. If the subject has been cubed, take the cube root.
❷ Divide both sides by the number now multiplying the subject.
❸ Rewrite the equation with the subject on the left.

● What to do if the subject occurs twice

➤ Q & A

Make x the subject of
$x + 6 = 3x + y$.

Answer

$x + 6 = 3x + y$

$6 = 2x + y$ [−x]

$2x + y = 6$ [rewrite]

$2x = 6 - y$ [−y]

$x = \dfrac{6 - y}{2}$ [÷2]

➤ Method
❶ Subtract the smallest subject term from both sides.
❷ Rewrite the equation with the remaining subject term on the left if necessary.
❸ Add/subtract any non-subject terms on the left to/from both sides.
❹ Divide both sides by the number now multiplying the subject.

---

1 Make q the subject of **a** $p = 4q^2$ **b** $p = 81q^2$.
2 Make a the subject of **a** $2a + 3b = a + 1$ **b** $a + 5b = 4a - b$.

TEST

Sequences & number patterns (1)

A <u>sequence</u> is a list of numbers that <u>follows a pattern</u> or rule.
Each number in a sequence is called a <u>term</u>.

● Adding or subtracting patterns

This is where a number is
added or subtracted to get
the next term in the sequence.

● Multiplying or dividing patterns

Here you multiply or divide
to get the next term.

● Square numbers

<u>Square numbers</u> are whole numbers <u>multiplied by themselves</u>.

$1 (1^2)$, $4 (2^2)$, $9 (3^2)$, $16 (4^2)$, $25 (5^2)$, ...

● Triangular numbers

Start at 1 and add 2, then 3,
then 4, then 5, ...

● *n*th term

The *n*th term is an expression used to find <u>any</u> term in a sequence.

> ➤ **Example**
>
> If someone tells you that the <u>*n*th</u> term of a sequence is <u>$3n + 4$</u>,
> then you can quickly work out any term in the sequence.
>
> The <u>1st</u> term is $3 \times \underline{1} + 4 = 7$,
> and the <u>100th</u> term is $3 \times \underline{100} + 4 = 304$.
>
> Just substitute the term
> number in place of *n*.

---

1 What is the next term in each of these sequences?
   a 5, 8, 11, 14, ...   **b** 3, 6, 12, 24, ...   **c** 21, 17, 13, 9, ...
2 How many squares are in the
   next diagram in the sequence?
3 The *n*th term of a sequence is $2n + 5$.
   Find these terms in the sequence:
   a 1st term   **b** 50th term   **c** 100th term

TEST

Sequences & number patterns (2)

● Finding the *n*th term of a linear sequence

Here the difference between consecutive terms is the same.

➤ Q & A

Find the *n*th term of this sequence: 6, 10, 14, 18, ...

Answer

❶ The difference between terms is 4.

❷ Write out the 4 times-table: 4, 8, 12, 16, ...

❸ The original sequence is always 2 more than the 4 times-table.

$$4 + 2, 8 + 2, 12 + 2, 16 + 2, ... \quad ⫸ \quad 6, 10, 14, 18, ...$$

This means that the *n*th term is 4*n* + 2.

The 4*n* gives the 4 times-table for *n* = 1, 2, 3, and so on.

The +2 is needed because the sequence is 2 more than the 4 times-table.

➤ Method

❶ Find the difference between the terms.

❷ Write out the times-table for the difference found in ❶.

❸ Compare the times-table to the original sequence.

● Quadratic sequences

If the difference between terms isn't constant, the sequence may be quadratic. This just means it's related to the sequence of square numbers: 1, 4, 9, 16, ...

➤ Q & A

Find the *n*th term of:
a 2, 5, 10, 17, ...
b 2, 8, 18, 32, ...

Answer

a These are the square numbers + 1, so *n*th term = $n^2 + 1$

b These are double the square numbers, so *n*th term = $2n^2$

➤ Method

❶ See what you would have to do to each term to get a square number.

❷ Do whatever you did to each term to n^2. You have found the *n*th term.

Tip: Always test your answer by calculating a few terms, e.g. in part **b** put in *n* = 1, 2, 3, 4 to get $2 \times 1^2 = 2$, $2 \times 2^2 = 8$, $2 \times 3^2 = 18$, $2 \times 4^2 = 32$. ✓

Find the *n*th term of each of these sequences.
a 7, 10, 13, 16, 19, ...   **b** 1, 5, 9, 13, 17, ...   **c** 4, 7, 12, 19, ...

TEST

28

Functions & mappings

A <u>function</u> (also called a <u>mapping</u>) changes an <u>input to an output</u>.

❶ Functions can be written in words, e.g.
<u>'multiply the input by 2 and then add 4 to get the output'</u>.

❷ Functions can be shown
by <u>function machines</u>:

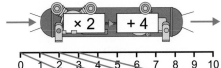

❸ Functions can be illustrated
by <u>mapping diagrams</u>:

❹ Functions can be described
using <u>algebra</u> (<u>letters</u>):

$x \longrightarrow 2x + 4$

● Inverse functions

An inverse function <u>reverses the</u>
<u>direction</u> of a mapping. This can
be shown in a mapping diagram.

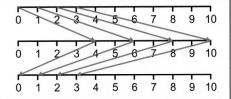

➤ Q & A

Find the inverse function of $x \to 2x + 4$.

Answer

Write the function as $y = 2x + 4$, then rearrange to get $x = \ldots$

$y - 4 = 2x$ [subtract 4 from both sides]

$(y - 4) \div 2 = x$ [divide both sides by 2]

$x = \frac{1}{2}y - 2$ [swap sides and remove brackets]

The final step is to write the function with x's only.

The inverse function is $x \to \frac{1}{2}x - 2$ (put inputs 4, 6, 8, 10 into this to see that it works)

---

1   a For this function machine, what
is the output when the input is 4?

    b What is the input when the output is 12?

    c Write the function machine as a function using algebra.

2   a Find the inverse function of $x \to 10 - x$.

    b What do you notice about your answer to part **a**?

TEST

Straight-line graphs (1)

● Plotting and drawing straight-line graphs

The secret to drawing graphs is to first construct a <u>table of values</u>.

➤ Q & A

Complete this table of values for the equation $y = 2x + 2$ and then draw its graph.

x	–2	–1	0	1	2
$y = 2x + 2$		0		4	

Answer

The missing values are when $x = -2$, $x = 0$ and $x = 2$.
Putting these values into the equation gives:

when $x = -2$: $y = 2x + 2 = 2 \times (-2) + 2 = -4 + 2 = \underline{-2}$
when $x = 0$: $y = 2x + 2 = 2 \times 0 + 2 = 0 + 2 = \underline{2}$
when $x = 2$: $y = 2x + 2 = 2 \times 2 + 2 = 4 + 2 = \underline{6}$

So the completed table is:

x	–2	–1	0	1	2
$y = 2x + 2$	–2	0	2	4	6

Next plot the points one at a time on graph paper:

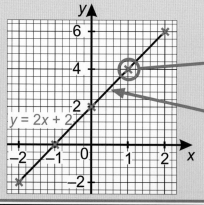

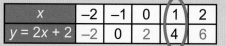

This pair of values gives the point (1, 4).

(1, 4) is plotted here.

Finally, use a <u>ruler</u> to draw a straight line through the points.

---

a Copy and complete the table of values for the equation: $y = 3x + 2$.

x	–2	–1	0	1	2
$y = 3x + 2$	–4			5	

b Draw the graph of $y = 3x + 2$ on graph paper.
(The x-axis should go from –2 to 2 and the y-axis should go from –4 to 8.)

TEST

Straight-line graphs (2)

● Finding the gradient of a straight line

> ### ➤ Method
> ❶ Pick two points on the line.
> ❷ Draw a triangle through the points.
> ❸ Work out the height of the triangle and the width of the triangle.
> ❹ Use this formula to work out the gradient of the line:
>
> $$\text{Gradient} = \frac{\text{height}}{\text{width}}$$

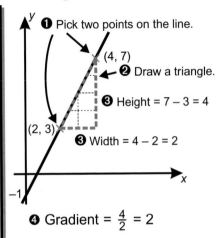

❶ Pick two points on the line.

(4, 7)

❷ Draw a triangle.

❸ Height = 7 – 3 = 4

(2, 3)

❸ Width = 4 – 2 = 2

❹ Gradient = $\frac{4}{2}$ = 2

● Positive or negative gradient?

If the graph slopes upwards (╱) the gradient will be positive.
If the graph slopes downwards (╲) the gradient will be negative.

● The general equation of a line is y = mx + c

All equations of straight lines can be written in the form $y = mx + c$.

m is the gradient. The greater the value of m the steeper the graph.
c is the y-intercept. This tells you the line cuts the y-axis at (0, c).

> ➤ The line above has gradient 2 and cuts the y-axis at y = –1.
> So the equation of the line is $y = 2x – 1$.

● Plotting other graphs

You might be asked to plot graphs other than straight lines.
These could involve squares or cubes, e.g. $y = 4x^2$ or $y = 2x^3 + 3x$.
As when plotting straight lines, you need to first draw up a table of values (basically work out y for different values of x).
See next page for the basic shapes of all the common graphs.

Write down the equation of the line that has gradient 5 and goes through the point (0, 4).

TEST

Graphs you should know

You need to be able to <u>recognise</u> all the graphs on this page.
You also need to be able to <u>sketch</u> them from their equations.

● Straight lines

Any graph with equation $y = mx + c$ is a <u>straight line</u>.

Make sure you can recognise these special cases:

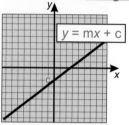

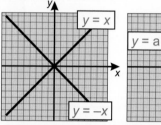

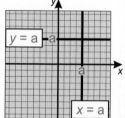

● Quadratics

Any graph with equation $y = ax^2 + bx + c$ is a <u>quadratic</u>.
You need to know what $y = x^2$ and $y = -x^2$ look like.

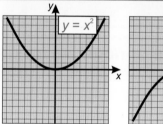

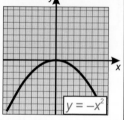

● Cubics

Cubics always have this basic shape:

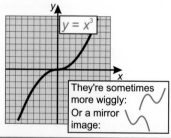

They're sometimes more wiggly: ∿ Or a mirror image: ∿

● Reciprocals

Reciprocals (a number over x) always have this basic shape:

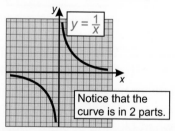

Notice that the curve is in 2 parts.

Cover the top part of this page. Sketch:

a $y = 3$ **b** $x = -5$ **c** $y = x$ **d** $y = -x$

e $y = x^2$ **f** $y = -x^2$ **g** $y = x^3$ **h** $y = \frac{1}{x}$

TEST

Speedy Revision

Real-life graphs

● Real-life straight-line graphs

The trick, again, is to first construct a <u>table of values</u>.

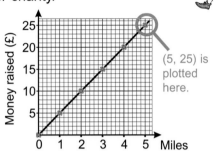

➤ Christina is taking part in a sponsored run. For every mile she runs she will raise £5 for her charity.

Miles run	Money raised
0	£0
1	£5
2	£10
3	£15
4	£20
5	£25

She raises £5 for 1 mile so she'll raise £5 × 5 = £25 for 5 miles.

(5, 25) is plotted here.

● Distance–time graphs

In a <u>distance–time graph</u> the <u>gradient</u> gives the <u>velocity</u> (speed).

➤ Q & A

The graph shows Suki's walk to and from a local shop. Describe her journey in words.

Answer

❶ She starts <u>walking slowly</u>.

❷ She <u>stops</u> for a short while, perhaps because she bumps into a friend.

❸ She starts <u>walking more quickly</u>.

❹ She <u>stops</u> in the shop for a while.

❺ She <u>walks home without stopping</u>.

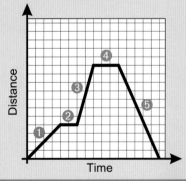

1 Describe the train journey shown in the graph.

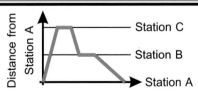

TEST

2 Calculate the gradient of the line in the sponsored run graph.

Inequalities (1)

➤ Q & A

List all the integer values of
n that satisfy $-2 \leqslant n < 3$.

Answer

$-2, -1, 0, 1, 2$

Include –2 because the first sign
means greater than or equal to –2.

Stop at 2 because the second
sign means less than 3.

The four inequality symbols

< means 'less than'.

≤ means 'less than or equal to'.

> means 'greater than'.

≥ means 'greater than or equal to'.

● Solving an inequality

You solve inequalities in exactly the same way as equations, with
one exception: if you multiply or divide by a negative number you
must reverse the inequality symbol. This can be tricky, so don't do it!
Follow the method below and you'll never have to.

➤ Q & A

Solve $4x + 1 > x - 5$.

Answer

$4x + 1 > x - 5$

$3x + 1 > -5$ [$-x$]

$3x > -6$ [-1]

$x > -2$ [$\div 3$]

➤ Method

❶ Get rid of the smallest x-term.
This will give you a positive
number of x on one side only.

❷ Add/subtract any numbers on
the x side to/from both sides.

❸ Divide both sides by the
number multiplying x.

● Showing inequalities on a number line

➤ Q & A

Show $x < -2$ and $0 \leqslant x < 5$ on a
number line.

Answer

Shade this circle because the
inequality was '≤', so 0 is included.

○ means not included

● means is included

Use arrows to show more
numbers are included.

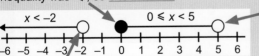

$x < -2$ $0 \leqslant x < 5$

–6 –5 –4 –3 –2 –1 0 1 2 3 4 5 6

Do not shade as the inequality
was '<', so 5 is not included.

Do not shade this circle as the inequality was '<', so –2 is not included.

See next page for TEST.

Speedy Revision

Inequalities (2)

● Showing inequalities on a graph

➤ Q & A

Shade the region on a graph that satisfies $y < x$ and $x \leqslant 5$.

Answer

First, plot the lines $y = x$ and $x = 5$.

Broken lines show points are not included (use if inequality was '<' or '>').

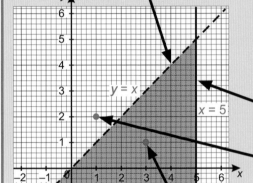

y = x

x = 5

➤ Method

❶ Replace the inequality symbols with '='.

❷ Draw the lines (plot a table of values or use $y = mx + c$).

❸ Pick a point (not on a line) and if it satisfies the original inequalities shade this region. If not try another point in a different region.

Solid lines show points are included (use for '≤' and '≥').

Pick a point, e.g. (1, 2), and see if it fits the inequalities:

$2 < 1$ and $2 \leqslant 5$ ✗

(1, 2) does not satisfy $y < x$.

So, pick another point, e.g. (3, 1), and see if it fits the inequalities:

$1 < 3$ and $3 \leqslant 5$ ✓   (3, 1) works, so shade the region it's in.

---

1 a List integer values of n that satisfy $-5 < n \leqslant 1$.

  b Show the solution to $-5 < n \leqslant 1$ on a number line.

2 a Solve $2x + 2 < x + 4$.

  b Show the solution on a number line.

3 Shade the region on a graph that satisfies $y > -2$ and $y \leqslant 2x$.

4 a Solve $10y - 5 \leqslant 6y + 3$.

  b Show the solution on a graph.

TEST

Simultaneous equations (1)

● Solving simultaneous equations graphically

Simultaneous equations are equations that are both true at the same time so you have to solve them both at the same time.

You can plot the graphs of the equations and read off the solution.

➤ Q & A

Solve graphically:

$y = x + 2$

$y = 4 - x$

Answer

You only need two points to draw a straight line, but plot three in case you make a mistake.

x	−2	0	2
$y = x + 2$	0	2	4
$y = 4 - x$	6	4	2

The graphs cross at (1, 3) so the solution is:

    $x = 1$ and $y = 3$

➤ Method

❶ Draw a table of values.
❷ Plot the graphs.
❸ Read off the x- and y-values where the graphs cross.

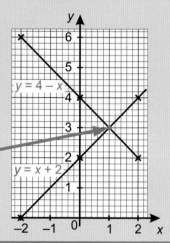

● There is no excuse for getting it wrong!

You should get these right every time, because you can check your answer – just pop the values from your answer back into the original equations to see if they work.

(Check the **Q & A** above by putting $x = 1$, $y = 3$ into $y = x + 2$ and $y = 4 - x$.)

---

1 Solve graphically:

   $y = x - 3$

   $y = 9 - 2x$

2 Solve graphically:

   $y = -x$

   $y = 3x - 4$

3 Why do $y = 2x + 3$ and $y = 2x - 1$ have no solution?

TEST

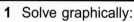 **Speedy** Revision

Simultaneous equations (2)

● Solving simultaneous equations algebraically

You don't have to draw a graph to solve simultaneous equations – you can solve them algebraically. Just remember that you're looking for <u>values of the two variables</u> (usually x and y) that <u>work in both equations</u>.

➤ Q & A

Solve algebraically:

$y = 6x - 16$

$2x + 3y = 12$

Answer

A	$-6x +$	y	$= -16$	$[-6x]$
B	$2x + 3y$		$= 12$	$[OK]$

C	$-6x +$	y	$= -16$	
D	$6x + 9y$		$= 36$	$[\times 3]$
		$10y$	$= 20$	$[C + D]$
		y	$= 2$	$[\div 10]$

➤ Method

❶ <u>Rewrite</u> both equations as $ax + by = c$. Label **A** and **B**.

❷ <u>Multiply</u> one (or both) of the equations by something to <u>get the same number in front of x (or y)</u> in both equations. Label **C** and **D**.

❸ <u>Add/subtract</u> one equation to/from the other to <u>eliminate x or y.</u>

❹ <u>Solve</u> this equation.

❺ <u>Substitute</u> this value into one of the <u>original</u> equations.

❻ <u>Solve</u> this equation.

$2x +$	6	$= 12$	[put $y = 2$ into **B**]
	$2x$	$= 6$	$[-6]$
	x	$= 3$	$[\div 2]$ <u>So the solution is $x = 3$ and $y = 2$.</u>

Check the answer by putting the $x = 3$ and $y = 2$ back into the original equations:

❼ <u>Check</u> your answer.

$y = 6x - 16$ ⟹ $(6 \times 3) - 16 = 2$ ✓

$2x + 3y = 12$ ⟹ $(2 \times 3) + (3 \times 2) = 12$ ✓

---

1 Solve algebraically:

$4x - 3y = 8$

$x + y = 9$

2 Solve algebraically:

$y = 2x + 6$

$3y - x = 8$

TEST

Trial & improvement

● Solving equations

Essential: you must show all your working.

➤ Q & A

The equation $x^3 + x = 75$ has a solution between 4 and 5. Use trial and improvement to find the solution to 2 d.p.

Answer

➤ Method

❶ Make a <u>sensible guess</u> for x and substitute it into the equation.

❷ If the left-hand side is <u>too big/small</u>, take a <u>smaller/ bigger guess</u>.

❸ Stop when you have two numbers that bound x and <u>round to the same number</u>.

x	$x^3 + x$		
4.5	95.625	too big	x is between 4 and 4.5
4.2	78.288	too big	x is between 4 and 4.2
4.1	73.021	too small	x is between 4.1 and 4.2
4.15	75.623375	too big	x is between 4.1 and 4.15
4.13	74.574997	too small	x is between 4.13 and 4.15
4.14	75.097944	too big	x is between 4.13 and 4.14

To see if the solution is 4.13 or 4.14 you need to try the <u>mid-value</u>:

4.135	74.83616...	too small	x is between 4.135 and 4.14

4.135 & 4.14 both round to 4.14, so the solution is <u>$x = 4.14$</u> to 2 d.p.

The last step in the **Q & A** can be seen clearly on a number line:

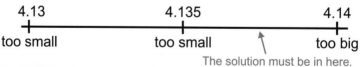

The solution must be in here.

● Finding roots

You can find values of roots, such as $\sqrt[3]{12}$, by trial and improvement. You start by taking a guess at the root. In the case of $\sqrt[3]{12}$, your first guess could be 2. Cubing this gives 8, which is smaller than 12 so you next guess needs to be bigger.

1 Find the solution of $x^3 - x = 50$ correct to 2 decimal places.
2 Find the value of $\sqrt[3]{12}$ correct to 1 decimal place.

TEST

Speedy Revision

Units of measurement & accuracy

● Metric units

Length: 1 km = 1000 m, 1 m = 100 cm, 1 cm = 10 mm
Mass: 1 tonne = 1000 kg, 1 kg = 1000 g
Capacity: 1 litre = 1000 ml, 1 litre = 100 cl, 1 cl = 10 ml, 1 ml = 1 cm^3

● Imperial units

Length: 1 yard (yd) = 3 feet (ft), 1 foot (ft) = 12 inches (in)
Mass: 1 stone (st) = 14 pounds (lb), 1 pound (lb) = 16 ounces (oz)
Capacity: 1 gallon (gal) = 8 pints (pt)

● Metric to imperial

Length: 1 mile ≈ 1.6 km, 1 m ≈ 39 in, 30 cm ≈ 1 ft, 2.5 cm ≈ 1 in
Mass: 1 kg ≈ 2.2 lb, 30 g ≈ 1 oz
Capacity: 1 pint ≈ 0.5 litre, 4.5 litres ≈ 1 gallon

● Accuracy of measurement

Measurements are often given to the <u>nearest whole unit</u>.
The measurement could really be up to <u>half a unit more or less</u> than the given value.

> ### Example
> A length is given as 17 cm to the nearest centimetre.
> This means that the actual length could be anywhere between 16.5 cm and 17.5 cm.
>
>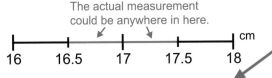
>
> The actual measurement could be anywhere in here.
>
> 'Less than' because length cannot equal 17.5 as this would have been rounded to 18 cm.
>
> As an inequality this is 16.5 ≤ length < 17.5.

Write down the upper and lower limits for these:
a 14 kg to the nearest kg   **b** 3 cm to the nearest mm

TEST

Angles & parallel lines

● Angle facts

An <u>acute angle</u> is less than 90°.

A <u>right angle</u> is 90°.

An <u>obtuse angle</u> is between 90° and 180°.

A <u>reflex angle</u> is more than 180°.

Angles on a straight line add up to 180°.

$$a + b = 180°$$

Angles at a point add up to 360°.

$$c + d + e + f = 360°$$

Vertically opposite angles are equal.

$p = r$ and $q = s$

● Parallel lines

Alternate angles are equal.

$u = v$

(The angles are in a Z-shape.)

Corresponding angles are equal.

$w = x$

(The angles are in an F-shape.)

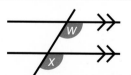

Work out the size of the lettered angles.

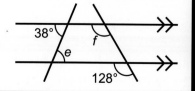

TEST

40

Speedy Revision

Polygons

- ### The angles in a triangle add up to 180°

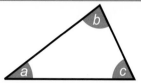

$$a + b + c = 180°$$

- ### The angles in a quadrilateral add up to 360°

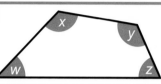

$$w + x + y + z = 360°$$

- ### Interior and exterior angles

The angles <u>inside</u> a polygon are called <u>interior angles</u>.

<u>Exterior angles</u> are found on the <u>outside</u> when the <u>sides are extended</u>.

<u>Learn</u> these two formulae:

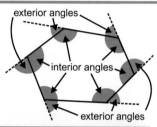
exterior angles
interior angles
exterior angles

❶ Sum of exterior angles = 360°

❷ Sum of interior angles = (number of sides – 2) × 180°

- ### Regular polygons

The <u>sides and angles</u> of a <u>regular polygon</u> are all the <u>same size</u>.

➤ Q & A

What is the size of an interior angle in a regular pentagon?

?

Answer

Using formula ❷ above we get:

Sum of interior angles of a regular pentagon = (5 – 2) × 180° = 540°

There are 5 equal interior angles, so size of one = 540° ÷ 5 = <u>108°</u>

---

1 Two interior angles of a triangle are 57° and 74°. What size is the other angle?

2 What size are the interior and exterior angles of
 a a square **b** a regular hexagon?

TEST

Symmetry

● Reflection symmetry

If a shape can be folded so that one half fits exactly on the other, it is said to have <u>reflection symmetry</u> (also known as <u>line symmetry</u>). Some shapes have more than one line of symmetry; some don't have any:

| Square | Equilateral triangle | No lines of symmetry |
| 4 lines of symmetry | 3 lines of symmetry | |

● Rotation symmetry

A shape has rotation symmetry if it looks exactly the same when turned. The <u>order of rotation symmetry</u> is the number of times a shape fits exactly over itself during a full-turn about its centre.

➤ **Q & A**

What is the order of rotation symmetry of these shapes?

Order 4   Order 3   Order 1

Note: Order of rotation symmetry 1 means <u>no rotation symmetry</u>.

● Plane symmetry

This is basically <u>reflection</u> symmetry in <u>3-D shapes</u>.
A plane of symmetry cuts a solid shape in half so that one half is the mirror image of the other.

➤ **Q & A**   Indicate one plane of symmetry in each shape.

Answer

Both of these shapes have more than one plane of symmetry. Can you see the others?

For each shape write down the: **i** number of lines of symmetry **ii** order of rotation symmetry.

a   **b**   **c** ⋔

TEST

42

Speedy Revision

Transformations (1)

A <u>transformation</u> maps the <u>object</u> (original shape) to an <u>image</u> (a new shape in a different position).

● Translation

A <u>translation</u> is defined by a <u>distance</u> and a <u>direction</u>.

A <u>vector</u> can be used to show the distance and direction.

➤ Q & A

a Describe the translation that takes A to B.

b Translate A by $\begin{bmatrix} -2 \\ -4 \end{bmatrix}$. Label the new shape A_1.

Answer

a A needs to move 6 left, 1 up to get to B. As a vector that's: $\begin{bmatrix} -6 \\ 1 \end{bmatrix}$

Use a <u>minus</u> to show moves <u>left</u> or <u>down</u>.

b $\begin{bmatrix} -2 \\ -4 \end{bmatrix}$

<u>Minus</u> 2 means <u>left</u> 2.

<u>Minus</u> 4 means <u>down</u> 4.

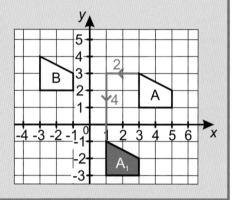

● Reflection   A <u>reflection</u> is defined by a <u>mirror line</u>.

➤ Q & A

Reflect A in the line $x = 1$.
Label the new shape A_2.

➤ Method

❶ Draw the <u>mirror line</u>.

❷ Draw lines from the corners of A to the mirror line <u>at right angles</u>.

❸ Draw the corners of A_2 the <u>same distance</u> from the mirror line.

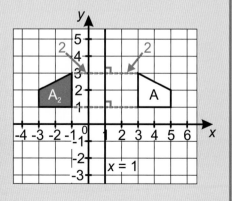

Transformations (2)

● Rotation

A <u>rotation</u> is defined by its <u>centre</u> and an <u>anticlockwise angle</u>.

These can be quite hard, so always use tracing paper to help you.

➤ Q & A

a Rotate A through 90°
about (3, 3).
Label the new shape A₃.

b Describe the rotation
that takes A to C.

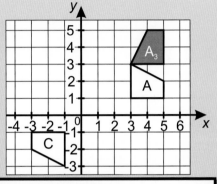

Answer

a

> ### ➤ Method for a
> ❶ <u>Trace</u> shape A.
> ❷ Put the point of your
> pencil on the centre of
> rotation and <u>rotate A
> anticlockwise</u> through
> the given angle.
> ❸ Draw and label A₃.

> ### ➤ Method for b
> ❶ <u>Guess</u> the centre of rotation.
> ❷ Use tracing paper and the
> method for **a** to <u>see if you
> are right</u>.
> ❸ If not, <u>keep guessing</u>.
> (Your guesses will improve
> with practice.)

b Rotation through 180°
about (1, 0)

---

1 Describe the transformation from P to
   a Q **b** R **c** S.

2 Copy the axes and shape Q.
   a Translate Q by $\begin{bmatrix} 5 \\ -2 \end{bmatrix}$.

   b Reflect Q in $y = x + 1$.

   c Rotate Q through 90°
   about (−1, 0).

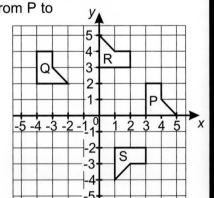

TEST

Speedy Revision

Transformations (3)

● Enlargement

An <u>enlargement</u> changes the <u>size</u> of an object, but not its shape.
To describe an enlargement you give its <u>centre</u> and <u>scale factor</u>.

▶ Q & A

a Enlarge A by a scale
factor of 2 about (–1, 1).
Label the image B.

b D is an enlargement of C.
Describe the enlargement.

Answer

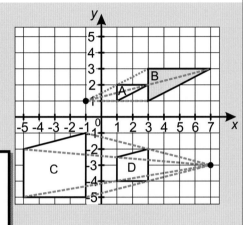

a

▶ Method for part a

❶ <u>Draw 'rays'</u> from the
centre of enlargement
through the vertices
of A.

❷ Draw the vertices of B
on these rays, <u>twice as
far</u> from the centre.

Twice as far, because
the scale factor is 2.

b Enlargement with
scale factor $\frac{1}{2}$,
centre (7, –3)

The scale factor is
a fraction because
the image is smaller
than the object.

▶ Method for part b

❶ <u>Draw 'rays'</u> through
corresponding vertices.
The point where these
cross is the <u>centre</u>.

❷ Measure <u>corresponding
lengths</u> to find the scale
factor.

---

1 Draw axes with both x and y from –10 to 10.
  a Plot these points. Join them in order. Label the shape A.
    (–5, –1), (–7, –5), (–5, –3), (–1, –5), (–5, –1)
  b Enlarge A using:
    i centre (–7, –9), s.f. 2 **ii** centre (–7, –9), s.f. $\frac{1}{2}$
2 Look again at the **Q & A**.
  Describe the transformation from **a** B to A **b** D to C.

TEST

Perimeter & circumference

● **Perimeter**

Perimeter is the distance around the outside edge of a 2-D shape. It is measured in mm, cm, m or km.

➤ **Q & A**

What is the perimeter of this shape?

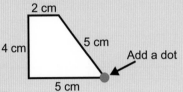

Answer

Start at the dot and add the sides up clockwise: $5 + 4 + 2 + 5 =$ 16 cm

➤ **Method**

❶ Mark a corner with a dot.

❷ Start at the dot, add the sides as you go around the shape. Stop when you get back to the dot.

❸ Essential: Show your working.

● **Circumference of a circle**

The circumference is the perimeter of a circle.

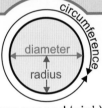

Circumference = π × diameter ($C = \pi d$)

$\pi \approx 3.14$ or 3.142 or press **π** (π is a Greek letter, pronounced 'pie'.)

➤ **Q & A**

This circle has a radius of 5 cm. What is its circumference?

Answer

The radius is 5 cm, so the diameter = 5 cm × 2 = 10 cm.

Circumference = π × diameter = 3.14 × 10 = 31.4 cm

➤ **Method**

❶ Find the diameter (the diameter is twice the radius).

❷ Use the formula: $C = \pi d$

TEST

1 Work out the perimeters of these shapes:

 a 10 cm, 4 cm

 b 2 cm, 2 cm, 10 cm, 4 cm

2 What is the circumference of a circle with radius 8 cm?

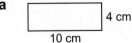 Revision

Areas of triangles & quadrilaterals

● **Area of a triangle**

Area = $\frac{1}{2}$ × base × height

$A = \frac{1}{2} \times b \times h$

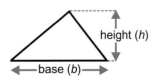

● **Area of a rectangle**

Area = length × width

$A = l \times w$

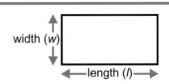

● **Area of a parallelogram**

Area = base × perpendicular height

$A = b \times h$

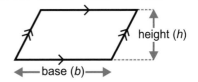

● **Area of a trapezium**

Area = $\frac{1}{2}$ × sum of parallel sides × height between them

$A = \frac{1}{2} \times (a + b) \times h$

Essential: for triangles, parallelograms and trapeziums make sure that you use the height that's at right angles to the base.

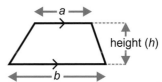

Memorise the formulae above (get someone to test you), then work out the areas of these shapes (remember your units):

a

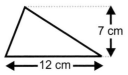

7 cm

12 cm

b

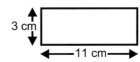

3 cm

11 cm

c

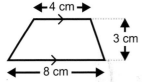

4 cm

3 cm

8 cm

d

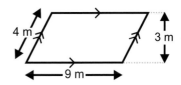

4 m

3 m

9 m

TEST

Areas of circles & composite shapes

● Area of a circle

Area = π × radius squared

$$A = \pi r^2$$

Use the **π** button (or π ≈ 3.14 or 3.142).

● Area of composite shapes

➤ Q & A

Work out the area of this shape:

Answer

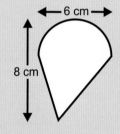

❶ The shape is a semicircle on top of a triangle.

❷ First, find the area of the semicircle:

Diameter is 6 cm, so the radius is 3 cm.

The area of a circle with radius 3 cm is π × 3² = 3.14 × 9 = 28.26 cm².

So the area of the semicircle is $\frac{1}{2}$ × 28.26 = 14.13 cm².

Next, work out the area of the triangle:

The height of the triangle is 8 – 3 = 5 cm. The base is 6 cm.

So the area of the triangle is $\frac{1}{2}$ × 5 × 6 = 15 cm².

❸ Total area of the shape = 14.13 cm² + 15 cm² = 29.13 cm²

➤ Method

❶ Split the shape into simple shapes.

❷ Work out the area of each simple shape.

❸ Add up the areas of the simple shapes to get the total area of the big shape.

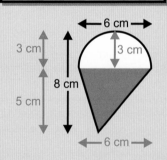

Work out the areas of these shapes:

a

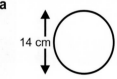

14 cm

b

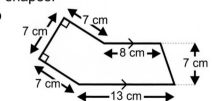

7 cm, 7 cm, 8 cm, 7 cm, 7 cm, 13 cm

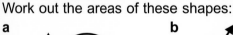

TEST

Speedy Revision

More circles

● Arcs & sectors

Learn these formulae for calculating the length of an arc and the area of a sector.

> Arc length = $\frac{\theta}{360} \times 2\pi r$
>
> Sector area = $\frac{\theta}{360} \times \pi r^2$

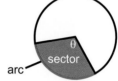

arc sector

> ➤ **Example**   Arc length $= \frac{90°}{360°} \times 2\pi r$
>
> $= 0.25 \times 2 \times \boxed{\pi} \times 5 = \underline{7.85 \text{ cm}}$
>
> Sector area $= \frac{90°}{360°} \times \pi r^2$
>
> $= 0.25 \times \boxed{\pi} \times 5^2 = \underline{19.6 \text{ cm}^2}$

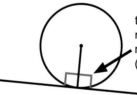

5 cm

Note: This is the <u>minor sector</u> (i.e. the small bit). The big bit is the <u>major sector</u>.

● Circle theorems

Make sure you know these <u>two facts</u> about circles.

❶ The <u>tangent</u> at any point on a circle is <u>perpendicular</u> to the <u>radius</u> at that point.

tangent and radius are at right angles (90°)

❷ A line drawn from the <u>centre</u> of a circle <u>perpendicular</u> to a chord <u>bisects the chord</u>.

AB = BC

The circle has a radius of 3 cm.

a Calculate the length of the grey arc.

b Calculate the area of the grey sector.

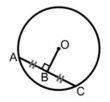

120°

TEST

Pythagoras' theorem (1)

- ### The square of the hypotenuse is equal to the sum of the squares of the other two sides

Using letters this is written as:

$$h^2 = a^2 + b^2$$

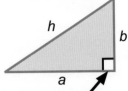

h is the <u>hypotenuse</u>, which is always the <u>longest side</u> (the side opposite the right angle).

Pythagoras' theorem only works in <u>right-angled</u> triangles.

- ### Finding h given a and b

➤ **Q & A**

What is the length of the hypotenuse?

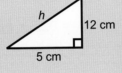

Answer

From the diagram: $\underline{a = 5, \ b = 12}$.

$h^2 = 5^2 + 12^2$

$\therefore h^2 = 25 + 144 = 169$

$\therefore h = \sqrt{169}$

$\therefore h = 13$

So the length of the hypotenuse is $\underline{13 \ cm}$.

➤ **Method**

❶ <u>Write down</u> the <u>values</u> of $\underline{a}$ and $\underline{b}$.

❷ Put these values into $h^2 = a^2 + b^2$.

❸ Find $\underline{h}$ by <u>solving the equation</u> (take the square root of both sides).

($\therefore$ means '<u>therefore</u>'.)

- ### Finding b given h and a

➤ **Q & A**

Find the missing length.

Answer

From the diagram: $\underline{h = 15, \ a = 9}$.

$15^2 = 9^2 + b^2$

$\therefore 225 = 81 + b^2$

$\therefore b^2 = 225 - 81 = 144$

$\therefore b = \sqrt{144}$

$\therefore b = 12$, so missing length is $\underline{12 \ cm}$.

➤ **Method**

❶ <u>Write down</u> the <u>values</u> of $\underline{h}$ and $\underline{a}$ (a is always the given side that isn't the hypotenuse).

❷ Put these values into $h^2 = a^2 + b^2$.

❸ Find $\underline{b}$ by <u>solving the equation</u>.

Pythagoras' theorem (2)

● Finding the distance between two points

➤ Q & A

Work out the distance between the points P(2, 1) and Q(5, 3).

Answer

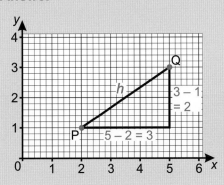

➤ Method

❶ Sketch the two points with a right-angled triangle drawn through them.

❷ Work out the lengths of the horizontal and vertical sides of the triangle (these are your a and b).

❸ Use $h^2 = a^2 + b^2$ to work out the hypotenuse (this is the distance between the two points).

From the diagram: $a = 3$, $b = 2$.

$h^2 = 3^2 + 2^2$ [put values into $h^2 = a^2 + b^2$]

∴ $h^2 = 9 + 4 = 13$

∴ $h = \sqrt{13}$

∴ $h = 3.6$ (to 1 d.p.)

So distance between P and Q is 3.6 units.

(You can use the ☑ button on your calculator to work out square roots.)

---

1 Use Pythagoras' theorem to work out the missing lengths. Give your answers to 1 d.p.

a
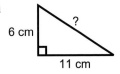
6 cm
?
11 cm

b
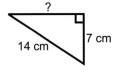
?
14 cm
7 cm

c
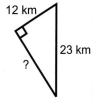
12 km
23 km
?

2 Work out the distance between these points:
a (4, 5) and (11, 13)   **b** (24, 11) and (12, −4)

3 Work out the coordinates of the midpoints of the lines between the points in **Q2**.
(Hint: add the x-coordinates then divide by 2, do the same for the y-coordinates.)

TEST

Trigonometry (1)

Trigonometry and Pythagoras' theorem both involve right-angled triangles.
The difference is that trigonometry involves angles. Pythagoras' only involves sides.

● Opposite & adjacent (& hypotenuse)

The first thing you should do when faced with a trig question is to label the sides of the triangle in relation to the angle you're interested in:

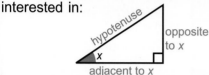

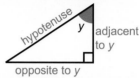

● Sine, cosine & tangent

$$\text{Sin } x = \frac{\text{Opposite}}{\text{Hypotenuse}} = \frac{O}{H}$$

$$\text{Cos } x = \frac{\text{Adjacent}}{\text{Hypotenuse}} = \frac{A}{H}$$

$$\text{Tan } x = \frac{\text{Opposite}}{\text{Adjacent}} = \frac{O}{A}$$

> A good way to learn the trig ratios is to remember this 'word':
>
> ## SOH-CAH-TOA
>
> Or you could make up a phrase to remember like 'Silly Old Harry Caught A Herring Trawling Off America'...

● Finding an angle given two sides

> ➤ **Q & A**

Work out the size of angle *w*.

Opp → 8 cm ← Hyp
5 cm
w
Adj

Answer

So Opp = 5 cm and Hyp = 8 cm.

SOH-CAH-TOA tells you that you need to use Sin, so:

$$\text{Sin } w = \frac{\text{Opp}}{\text{Hyp}} = \frac{5}{8} = 0.625$$

Now you have to find the inverse. You should have 0.625 on the screen

$(5 \div 8)$, so press [SHIFT] [sin] [=].

This gives *w* = 38.7°.

> ➤ **Method**
>
> ❶ Label sides Opp, Adj & Hyp in relation to the angle you want.
> ❷ Write down the two of Opp, Adj & Hyp you have been given.
> ❸ Use SOH-CAH-TOA to work out whether to use Sin, Cos or Tan.
> ❹ Find the inverse on your calculator.

Make sure you know how to find the inverse trig functions: $\sin^{-1}$, $\cos^{-1}$ and $\tan^{-1}$ on your calculator.

Speedy Revision

Trigonometry (2)

● Finding a side given an angle and another side

➤ Q & A

Work out the length of side AB.

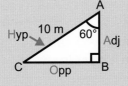

Answer

So Hyp = 10 m, and we need to find AB which is Adj.

SOH-CAH-TOA tells you that you need to use Cos:

$$\text{Cos } 60° = \frac{\text{Adj}}{\text{Hyp}}$$

$$\therefore \text{Cos } 60° = \frac{AB}{10}$$

$\therefore 10 \times \text{Cos } 60° = AB$ [×10]

$\therefore AB = 10 \times \text{Cos } 60°$ [swap sides]

Work this out on your calculator by pressing 【1】【0】【×】【cos】【6】【0】【=】.

This gives an answer of AB = <u>5 cm</u>.

Check this works on <u>your</u> calculator. You may have to press: 【1】【0】【×】【6】【0】【cos】【=】.

➤ Method

❶ Label sides Opp, Adj & Hyp in relation to the <u>angle you have been given</u>.

❷ Which of Opp, Adj & Hyp have you been given, and which do you have to find?

❸ Use SOH-CAH-TOA to work out whether to use Sin, Cos or Tan.

❹ Form an equation and solve it.

● Angles of elevation & depression

Angles of elevation or depression are measured from the horizontal up or down respectively.

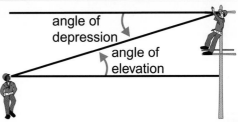

angle of depression

angle of elevation

---

1 Work out the size of the lettered angles and sides.

6 cm
10 cm
a

55° 13 cm
b

8 cm
38°
c

2 Lauren is 28 m from the base of a tree. The angle of elevation from ground level to the top of the tree is 35°. How tall is the tree? (Make a sketch then use trig.)

TEST

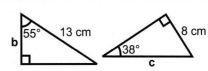

Volume & surface area (1)

● Volume

The <u>volume</u> of a 3-D solid is the <u>amount of space</u> it takes up.
It is measured in <u>mm³</u>, <u>cm³</u>, <u>m³</u> or <u>km³</u>. ← Notice the 'cubed' bit.

If the shape is made from cubes you can find the volume by <u>counting the cubes</u>. If not you'll have to use a <u>formula</u>:

● Volume of a cuboid

Volume = length × width × height

$V = l × w × h$

(This formula also works for a cube, i.e. $V = l × l × l = l^3$.)

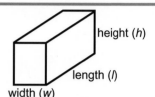
height (*h*)
length (*l*)
width (*w*)

● Volume of a prism

Volume = area of cross-section × length

$V = A × l$

(A prism is a shape with the same cross-section all along its length.)

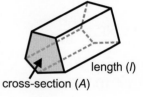
length (*l*)
cross-section (*A*)

➤ Q & A

Work out the volume of this triangular prism:

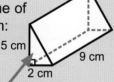
5 cm
9 cm
2 cm

Answer

The <u>area</u> of the <u>cross-section</u> (triangular end) is
$\frac{1}{2} × 2 × 5 = 5$ cm².

The <u>length</u> is 9 cm.

So <u>volume</u> = $A × l$ = 5 × 9 = <u>45 cm³</u>.

➤ Method

❶ Work out the <u>area</u> of the <u>cross-section</u>.

❷ Write down the <u>length</u> of the prism.

❸ Use the formula
$V = A × l$
to work out the volume.

❹ Remember your <u>units</u> (usually cm³ or m³).

● Volume of a cylinder

A cylinder is a prism with circular cross-section.

$V = \pi r^2 × h$

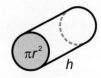
πr^2
h

Volume & surface area (2)

● Surface area

The <u>surface area</u> of a 3-D shape is the <u>total area</u> of all its <u>faces</u>.

➤ Q & A

Work out the surface area of
this cuboid.

Answer

First sketch the net of the cuboid.

The task now is to work out the area
of each of the six rectangles (faces).

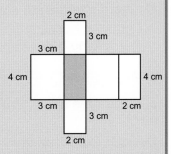

Two have an area of 2 cm × 3 cm = 6 cm^2
Two have an area of 2 cm × 4 cm = 8 cm^2
Two have an area of 3 cm × 4 cm = 12 cm^2

So the total surface area is
6 + 6 + 8 + 8 + 12 + 12 = <u>52 cm^2</u>.

● Changing units

➤ Q & A

The volume of a cupboard is 4.5 m^3.
What is the volume in cm^3?

Answer

4.5 m^3

= 4.5 (100 cm)^3 [1 m = 100 cm]

= 4.5 × 100^3 cm^3

= 4.5 × 1 000 000 cm^3

= <u>4 500 000 cm^3</u>

➤ Method

❶ Write the area/volume down.

❷ Write it again with the <u>new length unit</u> in place of the <u>old length unit</u>.

❸ <u>Square</u> (for area) or <u>cube</u> (for volume) the new length unit.

❹ Multiply the numbers.

To go from cm^3 to m^3, divide by 100^3.

---

1 Work out the volume & surface area of each of these shapes:

a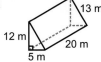

b

c

TEST

2 Change the units in your answer in **1a** to cm^3 and cm^2 & **1c** to m^3 and m^2.

Dimensions

● Length, area or volume?

The <u>dimensions</u> of a formula are the <u>number of lengths multiplied together</u> in each term.

❶ <u>Length</u> has <u>1 dimension</u>.

❷ <u>Area</u> terms are always <u>length × length</u>, so area has <u>2 dimensions</u>.

❸ <u>Volume</u> terms are always <u>length × length × length</u>, so volume has <u>3 dimensions</u>.

➤ Example

❶ l, w and h are lengths.

❷ hw, lw and hl are all areas (of faces).

❸ lwh is the volume.

➤ Q & A

p, q and r are all lengths.

Decide whether each expression is a length, area, volume or none of these.

➤ Method

❶ <u>Look at the first term</u>. Is it length, length × length or length × length × length? (Remember: length^2 means length × length.)

❷ <u>Check the other terms</u> are the same. If an expression is, e.g. length + area, it isn't a length or an area.

Answer

Expression	Type
$p + q$	<u>Length (2 terms, both lengths)</u>
3	<u>None (numbers have no dimensions)</u>
$10pq$	<u>Area (ignore any numbers multiplying lengths)</u>
$p + 2r$	<u>Length</u>
$8pr^2$	<u>Volume</u>
$q^2 + r^2$	<u>Area</u>
$pq + 5r$	<u>None (area + length)</u>
$pqr + p^3$	<u>Volume</u>

I've just come from another dimension.

Are these lengths, areas or volumes? (All letters are lengths.)

a $10a^2$　**b** $xyz + 2$　**c** $pq + qr + rs$　**d** π　**e** $3u + 5t$　**f** $c^2d + cd^2$

TEST

Congruent & similar shapes (1)

● Similar shapes

Similar shapes are exactly the same shape.

Congruent shapes are exactly the same shape *and* size.

➤ Q & A

Which of these are similar, congruent or neither?

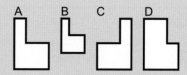

Answer

A and C are similar to B. A is congruent to C. D is neither.

● Similar shapes are enlargements of each other

➤ Q & A

These two triangles are similar. Calculate the missing lengths.

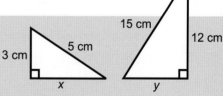

Answer

Use the hypotenuses to find the scale factor.

$$5 \text{ cm} \xrightarrow{\times 3} 15 \text{ cm}$$

So the s.f. is 3.

y is the shortest side so it corresponds to 3 cm:

$y = 3 \text{ cm} \times 3 = \underline{9 \text{ cm}}$ ◄

That leaves x and 12 cm:

$x = 12 \text{ cm} \div 3 = \underline{4 \text{ cm}}$ ◄

➤ Method

❶ Use the common length to find the scale factor (s.f.) that takes you from the small triangle to the large one.

❷ Multiply/divide by the s.f. to find the missing lengths.

Multiply when you are going from the small triangle to the large one.

Divide when going from large to small.

---

1 Are these similar, congruent or neither?

  a A and B   **b** A and C

2 D is similar to B.
  Find x.

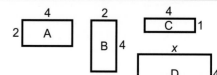

TEST

Congruent & similar shapes (2)

● Areas and volumes of similar shapes

When the <u>lengths</u> in a shape are enlarged by a <u>scale factor k</u>:
◆ the <u>area</u> is enlarged by <u>scale factor k^2</u>
◆ the <u>volume</u> is enlarged by <u>scale factor k^3</u>.

➤ Examples

A square that is enlarged by <u>scale factor 4</u>, will have sides 4 times longer, but an area $4^2 = 16$ times larger.

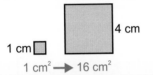

1 cm
1 cm² ➜ 16 cm²

4 cm

A cube that is enlarged by <u>scale factor 3</u>, will have sides 3 times longer, but a volume $3^3 = 27$ times larger.

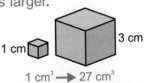

1 cm
3 cm
1 cm³ ➜ 27 cm³

● Congruent triangles

Two triangles are congruent if one of these conditions is true:

SSS Three pairs of sides are equal. 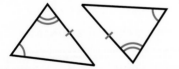	**SAS** Two pairs of sides are equal and the angle between them is equal. 
AAS Two pairs of angles are equal and one pair of corresponding sides are equal.	**RHS** Both triangles have a right angle, the hypotenuses are equal and one pair of corresponding sides is equal. 

---

1 The ratio of the radii of two spheres is 1 : 4. Calculate the ratio of **a** the surface areas **b** the volumes of the spheres.

2 Write down the four conditions for congruent triangles. (Close this page first, obviously ...)

TEST

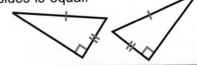 **Speedy** Revision

Bearings & scale drawings

● Bearings

❶ A bearing is <u>an angle</u> that gives a <u>direction</u>.
❷ Bearings are measured <u>clockwise</u> from the <u>North line</u>.
❸ All bearings are given as <u>3 figures</u>.

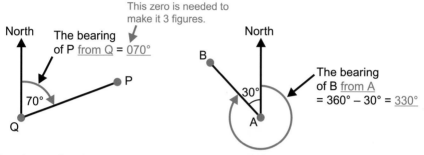

This zero is needed to make it 3 figures.

North
The bearing of P <u>from Q</u> = <u>070°</u>
P
70°
Q

North
B
30°
The bearing of B <u>from A</u> = 360° – 30° = <u>330°</u>
A

Look out for the word <u>from</u>; it tells you where to draw the North line and measure <u>from</u>.

● Scale drawings & maps

Scale drawings usually have a scale something like '<u>1 cm = 5 m</u>'.
This means that a length of <u>1 cm on the drawing</u> represents a
distance of <u>5 m in real life</u>. A scale can also be given as a <u>ratio</u>, e.g.
1 cm = 5 m can be written as <u>1 : 500</u>.

➤ Example

The map shows the positions of three towns.

The distance between Berlham and Carwick is <u>3 cm</u> on the map.

The scale is <u>1 cm = 20 km</u>, so this means that the distance in real life is <u>20 km × 3 = 60 km</u>.

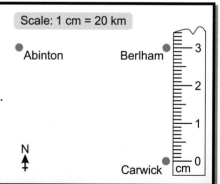

Scale: 1 cm = 20 km

Abinton   Berlham
3
2
1
N
0
Carwick cm

---

1 In the example above, what is the bearing of:
  a Berlham from Abinton **b** Abinton from Berlham?
2 What is the distance in real life between Abinton and Carwick?

TEST

Compound measures

● **Speed =** $\dfrac{\textbf{Distance}}{\textbf{Time}}$

There are 3 ways of writing this formula:

$S = \dfrac{D}{T}$ $T = \dfrac{D}{S}$ $D = S \times T$

All 3 ways can be remembered using this 'formula triangle':

➤ **Q & A**

A car travels at 70 mph for 2.5 hours. How far does it go?

Answer

Distance is needed so cover up D.

This gives D = S × T

D = 70 × 2.5 = 175

The car travels 175 miles.

➤ **Method**

❶ Cover up what you want on the formula triangle. Write down the formula this gives.

❷ Write the formula with the numbers you know. (Make sure the units match. e.g. if the speed has hours in it, the time must be in hours.)

❸ Calculate the answer.

● **Density =** $\dfrac{\textbf{Mass}}{\textbf{Volume}}$

Like the one for speed, this formula can also be written in a 'formula triangle': ➤

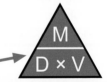

➤ **Q & A**

A block has a density of 22 kg/m³. The mass of the block is 88 kg. What is the volume of the block?

Answer

Volume is needed so cover up V.

This gives V = $\dfrac{M}{D}$

So V = $\dfrac{88}{22}$ = 4

The block has a volume of 4 m³.

---

1 How long will a car travelling at 60 km/h take to travel 40 km?

2 Calculate the mass of 2 m³ of wood of density 500 kg/m³.

TEST

Speedy Revision

Constructions & loci (1)

● How to construct an equilateral triangle

❶

Draw a line of the length you want the sides to be, e.g. 5 cm.

❷

Set your compasses to 5 cm. Draw two crossing arcs from the ends of the line.

❸

You've also constructed an angle of 60°.

Join the point where the arcs crossed to the ends of the line.

● Perpendicular bisector of a line

Perpendicular means 'at right angles'. Bisect means 'cut in half'.

This is similar to constructing an equilateral triangle.

You just have to draw two more crossing arcs on the other side of the line.

Set your compasses to more than half the length of the line.

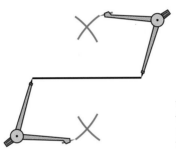

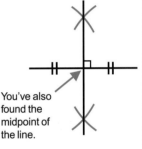

You've also found the midpoint of the line.

● Perpendicular from a point to a line

❶ Draw two arcs on the line, centred on the point. Keep your compasses set at the same distance.

❷ Draw two crossing arcs on the other side of the line, with the compasses centred on the arcs on the line.

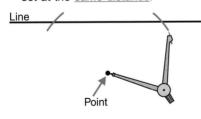

Line

Point

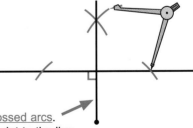

❸ Draw a line from the point to the crossed arcs. This is the perpendicular from the point to the line.

---

1 Construct an equilateral triangle of side 6 cm.
2 Draw a line 8 cm long. Construct its perpendicular bisector.
3 Construct the perpendicular from a point to a line.

TEST

Constructions & loci (2)

● Perpendicular from a point on a line

❶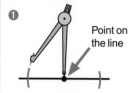
Point on the line

❷

❸

Draw arcs on the line either side of the point. Use the same radius.

Increase the radius. Draw two crossing arcs centred on the arcs on the line.

Join the original point to where the arcs crossed. This is the perpendicular.

● Bisector of an angle

❶

❷

❸
The line cuts the angle in half.

Draw two arcs on the arms of the angle, centred on the vertex.

Draw two crossing arcs inside the angle, centred on the arcs on the arms.

Join the vertex to the point where the arcs crossed.

● Loci

A locus is a set of points (often lines) that satisfy a given rule. Here are four loci that you should know (loci are in colour):

❶

❷

❸

❹

A fixed distance from a point is a circle.

A fixed distance from a straight line is two parallel straight lines.

Equidistant from two points is the perpendular bisector of the line joining the two points.

Equidistant from two straight lines is the bisectors of the angles between the lines.

Types ❶ & ❷ are often combined:

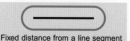
Fixed distance from a line segment

---

1 Construct a perpendicular 5 cm from the end of a 14 cm line.
2 Draw a 68° angle with a protractor. Bisect it with compasses.
3 Construct the locus of points 4 cm from a line 6 cm long.

Speedy Revision

Mean, median, mode, range (1)

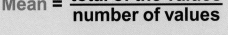
You need to learn these.

Mean = $\dfrac{\text{total of the values}}{\text{number of values}}$

Median = the middle value when the numbers are put in order of size

Mode = the most common value

Range = highest value – lowest value

When people talk about 'the average' they're usually referring to 'the mean'. But be careful, because the median and mode are also 'averages'.

▶ Q & A

Find the mean, median, mode and range of this set of data:

5, 2, 3, 1, 5, 5, 10, 2, 3

Answer

Mean
The total of the values = 5 + 2 + 3 + 1 + 5 + 5 + 10 + 2 + 3 = 36
The number of values = 9 (count the numbers in the list)
So the mean = 36 ÷ 9 = 4.

Median
Rearrange the numbers in order of size.
1, 2, 2, 3, 3, 5, 5, 5, 10
The middle number is 3, so the median = 3.

Mode
The most common value is 5 (there are three of them). So the mode = 5.

> If there are an even number of values, the median is halfway between the middle two.
> e.g. the median of 2, 3, 4, 5 is (3 + 4) ÷ 2 = 3.5.

Range
The highest value = 10 and the lowest value = 1.
So the range = 10 – 1 = 9.

Find the mode, median, mean and range of this set of data:
5, 6, 7, 4, 4, 12, 4

TEST

Mean, median, mode, range (2)

● Using the appropriate average

- The mean is useful as it takes all the values into account, but it can be distorted by extreme values, e.g. you wouldn't use the mean for this data: 1, 2, 2, 3, 5, 909.
- The median is useful when there are extreme values (as in the above example).
- The mode is useful when you just want the most common value, e.g. the week's best selling DVD.

● Comparing sets of data

When comparing two sets of data you should use one of the 'averages' and the range.

➤ Q & A

Jane scored a mean of 2.9 goals per game last season and had a range of 4 − 2 = 2. David scored a mean of 3.1 goals per game and had a range of 5 − 0 = 5. Which player would you pick for the team?

Answer

Although David's mean score is higher, Jane's lower range shows that she scores more consistently. So you would probably want to pick Jane, but you could pick David if you wanted a riskier strategy.

Discrete & continuous data

● Discrete data

Discrete data can only take certain values and is often found by counting.
For example, the number of candles on a cake.

● Continuous data

Continuous data can take any value in a given range and is often found by measuring.
For example, the mass of rubbish in a bin.

Are these discrete or continuous data?
a The heights of students   **b** The number of people on a bus

Collecting data & two-way tables

● Collecting data

Two ways of collecting data are by:

❶ Observation: e.g. noting the colour of cars in a car park. Here you need to use a data collection sheet. This will often look like a simple tally/frequency chart (see page 66).

> Primary data is data you collect yourself.
>
> Secondary data is data that other people have collected.

❷ Questionnaire: Here you ask people suitable questions, e.g. 'What colour car do you drive?'

- Don't ask for information that is not needed, e.g. don't ask for a person's age if your survey doesn't need it.
- Make sure your question isn't leading (biased), e.g. never start a question 'Do you agree that ... ?'
- Allow for all possible answers. Using tick boxes is a good idea.

How many times have you been on an aeroplane?
Never ☐   1 to 2 ☐   3 to 4 ☐   5 & over ☐

● Two-way tables

Two-way tables show two sets of information in the one table.

> **Example** This two-way table shows the number of DVDs and CDs owned by a group of friends.

	DVDs	CDs	Total
Boys own	2	9	11
Girls own	18	31	49
Total	20	40	60

Boys own 9 CDs

Girls own 18 DVDs

There is a total of 60 DVDs and CDs

1 What is wrong with this survey question?
How many dogs do you own?   None ☐   2 or more ☐

2 Complete this two-way table that shows the colours of pens owned by a group of friends.

	Black	Red	Blue	Total
Boys own	14		11	26
Girls own	7	7		34
Total	21	8	31	60

TEST

Speedy Revision

65

Frequency tables (1)

● Frequency tables

Frequency tables display data that has been counted.

If you are given a long list of numbers, you can group the numbers into intervals such as $20 \leqslant n < 30$.

For example, this list:
22, 14, 15, 23, 33, 14,
37, 36, 22, 25, 31, 6,
13, 8, 23, 23, 30, 20
is shown in the
frequency table.

Note: 20 belongs to $20 \leqslant n < 30$, not $10 \leqslant n < 20$.

Number, n	Tally	Frequency
$0 \leqslant n < 10$	||	2
$10 \leqslant n < 20$	||||	4
$20 \leqslant n < 30$	⦀⦀ ||	7
$30 \leqslant n < 40$	⦀⦀	5
Total		18

● Frequency diagrams

Frequency diagrams show grouped continuous data.

The bars touch.

The diagram shows the data from the **Q & A** on page 67.

Make sure the bars have equal widths.

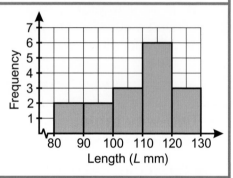

● Frequency polygons

A frequency polygon is a line graph of frequency against midpoint of the groups.

Joining the tops of the frequency diagram bars is the easiest way to draw a frequency polygon.

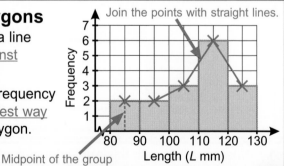

Join the points with straight lines.

Midpoint of the group

---

1 Show this data in a frequency table (group as in e.g. above):
   20, 12, 3, 45, 32, 9, 12, 5, 23, 25, 32, 31, 40, 32, 12, 33
2 For the height data in the TEST on page 67, draw
   a a frequency diagram **b** a frequency polygon.

TEST

Speedy Revision

Frequency tables (2)

● Estimating the mean from grouped data

You don't have the raw data, so you can only <u>estimate</u> the mean.

➤ Q & A

The table shows the lengths of candles on a birthday cake.
Estimate the mean length.

Answer

➤ Method

❶ Add a <u>column of midpoints</u>.
❷ <u>Multiply</u> each <u>midpoint</u> by its <u>frequency</u>.
❸ <u>Total</u> this column.
❹ <u>Divide</u> by the <u>total frequency</u>.

Length (L mm)	Frequency	Midpoint	Freq. × midpoint
$80 \leqslant L < 90$	2	85	170
$90 \leqslant L < 100$	2	95	190
$100 \leqslant L < 110$	3	105	315
$110 \leqslant L < 120$	6	115	690
$120 \leqslant L < 130$	3	125	375
Total	16	Total	1740

Estimated mean = 1740 ÷ 16 = <u>109 mm</u> (to nearest mm)

● Median

You can't give an exact value for the <u>median</u>, but you can say which <u>group it's in</u>.

➤ The median is the 8.5th value, which is in the $110 \leqslant L < 120$ group.

● Modal group

The <u>modal group</u> has the <u>highest frequency</u>.

➤ The modal group is $110 \leqslant L < 120$.

These are the heights (h cm) of 20 students:
152, 167, 169, 158, 177, 165, 172, 168, 156, 161,
163, 166, 171, 157, 162, 169, 168, 155, 176, 167

a Put the data into a frequency table with groups
$150 \leqslant h < 155$, $155 \leqslant h < 160$, ... (Use tallies to help you.)
b Use the table to calculate an estimate for the mean.
c Which group is the median in? **d** Which is the modal group?

TEST

Stem & leaf diagrams; line graphs

● Stem & leaf diagrams

These are like <u>bar charts</u>, but each bar displays the <u>actual data</u>.

➤ Q & A

Show this data on a stem and leaf diagram.

4, 5, 8, 12, 18, 19, 20, 22, 24, 25, 25, 26, 31, 32, 34, 36, 40, 43, 44

Answer

The 'stem' is the first part of the number, in this case Tens.

0	4 5 8
1	2 8 9
2	0 2 4 5 5 6
3	1 2 4 6
4	0 3 4

Always include a key.➝ Key: 1 | 8 means 18

The 'leaf' is the rest of the number, in this case Units.

The <u>leaves</u> should be given in <u>order of size</u>. If the original list of data had been jumbled you would have had to re-order the leaves.

● Line graphs

A line graph is a set of <u>points joined with straight lines</u>.

This type of graph is very good for showing <u>trends</u> over periods of <u>time</u> (they are sometimes called 'time series').

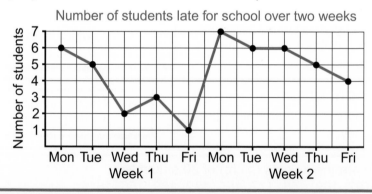

Number of students late for school over two weeks

---

1 30 students got these marks in a test:

50, 75, 51, 68, 72, 48, 62, 58, 65, 62, 42, 70, 54, 67, 60, 73, 74, 69, 62, 59, 63, 72, 62, 63, 57, 69, 49, 56, 58, 70

Draw a stem and leaf diagram to show the data.

2 Describe any trends you can see in the line graph above.

TEST

Speedy Revision

Scatter graphs

● Plotting scatter graphs

This table shows some students' results for two maths tests.

Test 1	5	8	9	11	15	17	19
Test 2	5	9	12	14	16	18	20

You can <u>plot the points</u> on a graph – this is a <u>scatter graph</u>.

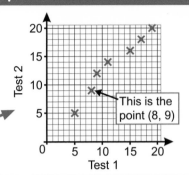

This is the point (8, 9)

● Line of best fit

This is a line drawn on a <u>scatter graph</u> that shows the <u>general direction</u> of the points.

You should try to get the <u>same</u> number of points <u>above</u> the line as <u>below</u>.

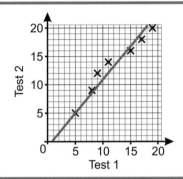

● Correlation

This is a fancy way of saying whether the points are related or not:

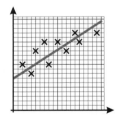

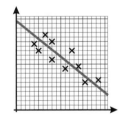

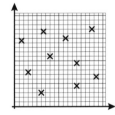

Positive correlation (╱)
<u>Strong</u> if the points lie <u>close to a straight line</u>, otherwise <u>weak</u>.

Negative correlation (╲)
<u>Strong</u> if the points lie <u>close to a straight line</u>, otherwise <u>weak</u>.

No correlation
The points seem to be <u>randomly</u> positioned.

Show the data as a scatter diagram.
Describe the correlation.

Age (years)	1	6	4	4	10	3	8	7	9
Value (£)	45	18	28	24	4	37	10	17	9

TEST

Cumulative frequency (1)

The <u>cumulative frequency</u> (C.F.) is the <u>running total</u> of frequency up to the <u>end of the group</u>. You always plot it at the <u>end of the group</u>.

➤ Q & A

These are the weights of wheelie bins in a street.

Weight (W kg)	Frequency
$0 \leqslant W < 5$	5
$5 \leqslant W < 10$	12
$10 \leqslant W < 15$	27
$15 \leqslant W < 20$	14
$20 \leqslant W < 25$	2

Draw a cumulative frequency graph.

Answer

Add a 3rd column to the table to work out the C.F.s:

Cumulative frequency
5
5 + 12 = 17
17 + 27 = 44
44 + 14 = 58
58 + 2 = 60

Think of cumulative frequency as the '<u>running total</u>'.

➤ Method

❶ Calculate the <u>C.F.s</u>.

❷ Draw a <u>horizontal axis</u> for the <u>end-points</u> of the groups. Draw a <u>vertical axis</u> for <u>C.F.</u>

❸ Plot each <u>C.F.</u> against the group <u>end-point</u>.

❹ Join the points with a <u>smooth curve</u>.

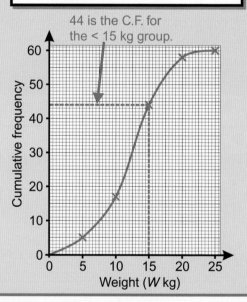

44 is the C.F. for the < 15 kg group.

● Reading from the graph

You can use the graph to find out how many wheelie bins weigh more or less than a particular weight.

➤ Example

The C.F. for 18 kg is 54. This means that 54 bins weigh up to 18 kg.

Check this on the graph by drawing a line up from 18 kg to the curve. Then draw a line across to the cumulative frequency axis. Go on!

Cumulative frequency (2)

● Median, quartiles & interquartile range

The median is halfway through the distribution.

The lower quartile (LQ) is a quarter of the way through.

The upper quartile (UQ) is three-quarters of the way through.

> Interquartile range (IQR) = upper quartile – lower quartile

➤ Q & A

Use the cumulative frequency graph to find

a the median

b the interquartile range.

Answer

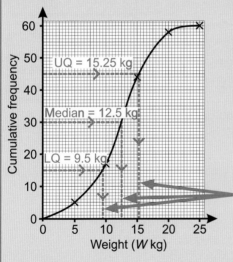

➤ Method

❶ Decide how far up the C.F. axis you need to go: halfway for the median, a quarter of the way for the LQ, three-quarters of the way for the UQ.

❷ Draw a horizontal line to the C.F. curve.

❸ Draw a vertical line down to the other axis.

❹ Read off the value.

The total C.F. is 60, so
the median has C.F. = 60 ÷ 2 = 30,
the LQ has C.F. = 60 ÷ 4 = 15,
the UQ has C.F. = 60 ÷ 4 × 3 = 45.

Now, read off the values for the median, UQ and LQ from the graph.

a Median = 12.5 kg   **b** IQR = UQ – LQ = 15.25 – 9.5 = 5.75 kg

---

Plot the cumulative frequency curve for these TV prices. Use it to find the median, lower and upper quartiles, and the interquartile range.

TV price (£P)	150–	200–	250–	300–	350–
Frequency	3	8	12	6	1

TEST

Probability (1)

<u>Probabilities</u> can be given as <u>fractions or decimals</u>, but they are always <u>between 0 and 1</u>. If something has <u>probability 0</u> it <u>can't happen</u>; if it has <u>probability 1</u> it will <u>definitely happen</u>.

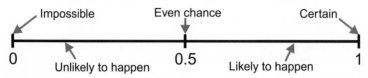

Impossible   Even chance   Certain

0   Unlikely to happen   0.5   Likely to happen   1

● **Theoretical probability**

$$P(\text{event}) = \frac{\text{No. of ways event can occur}}{\text{No. of possible outcomes}}$$

<u>P(event)</u> is a short way of writing '<u>the probability of an event happening</u>'.

> ➤ **Example**
> If an ordinary dice is rolled:
> $P(6) = \frac{1}{6}$
> $P(\text{even}) = \frac{3}{6} = \frac{1}{2}$

● **Mutually exclusive**

Outcomes are <u>mutually exclusive</u> if they <u>can't happen at the same time</u>.

> ➤ **Example**
> You can't get a head *and* a tail when you toss a coin.

Learn these important rules for mutually exclusive events:

❶ P(Not A) = 1 – P(A)   ❷ P(A or B) = P(A) + P(B)

➤ **Q & A**

There are 6 blue, 4 yellow, 3 black and 2 green beads in a bag.
A bead is picked at random. What is the probability that it is
a blue **b** yellow **c** not blue **d** blue or yellow?

Answer

a $P(\text{blue}) = \frac{6}{15} = \frac{2}{5}$

b $P(\text{yellow}) = \frac{4}{15}$

c $P(\text{not blue}) = 1 - P(\text{blue}) = 1 - \frac{2}{5} = \frac{3}{5}$

d $P(\text{blue or yellow}) = P(\text{blue}) + P(\text{yellow}) = \frac{6}{15} + \frac{4}{15} = \frac{10}{15} = \frac{2}{3}$

Probability (2)

● Experimental probability

You can carry out trials to estimate probability, e.g. rolling a dice lots of times.

$$\text{Estimated probability} = \frac{\text{Number of successful trials}}{\text{Total number of trials}}$$

The more trials, the better the estimate.

➤ Q & A

Here are the results of rolling a dice 100 times.

Number	1	2	3	4	5	6
Frequency	16	17	20	13	15	19

Estimate the probability of getting a 5.

Answer

$P(5) = \frac{15}{100} = \frac{3}{20}$

➤ Method

❶ Use the formula to calculate the probability.

❷ Simplify if possible.

● Independent events

If you roll a fair dice twice, the number you get the first time doesn't affect the number you get the second time. These are independent events.

For independent events A and B:

$P(A \text{ and } B) = P(A) \times P(B)$

➤ Q & A

A coin is tossed twice. What is the probability of getting two heads.

Answer

$P(H \text{ and } H) = P(H) \times P(H) = \frac{1}{2} \times \frac{1}{2} = \frac{1}{4}$

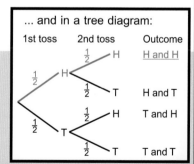

... and in a tree diagram:

1st toss	2nd toss	Outcome

H and H
H and T
T and H
T and T

TEST

1 Two dice are rolled and the scores multiplied. Find the probability of getting an even product. (Hint: draw a table.)
2 A card is picked at random from an ordinary pack of cards. What is the probability that it is:
   a a Spade   **b** not a King   **c** a red card or the Ace of Spades?
3 Two fair dice are rolled. What's the probability of a double 6?

Speedy revision test (1)

These questions test the basic facts. The simple truth is that the more of them you can answer, the better you'll do in your SATs. So try them as often as you can. (The answers can be found on the pages given at the end of each question.)

1 What is a multiple? What is a factor? (p4)

2 What are the first seven prime numbers? (p4)

3 Write 20 as a product of its prime factors. (p4)

4 How do you find the LCM of two numbers? How about the HCF? (p5)

5 Round **a** 0.168 to two decimal places **b** 5384 to two significant figures. (pp6–7)

6 Write $\frac{15}{45}$ in its simplest form. (p8)

7 Work out **a** $\frac{2}{3} + \frac{1}{5}$ **b** $\frac{3}{4} \times \frac{5}{7}$ **c** $\frac{2}{9} \div \frac{3}{7}$. (pp8–9)

8 Reduce £37.50 by 25%. (p10)

9 What is the formula for 'Percentage change'? (p11)

10 Write these as fractions: **a** 75% **b** 0.12 (p12)

11 What should you do first when ordering fractions, decimals & percentages? (p13)

12 Divide £120 in the ratio 2 : 3. (p14)

13 What are the two rules for multiplying and dividing negative numbers? (p15)

14 What is any non-zero number to the power of zero? (p16)

15 What is any number to the power of one? (p16)

16 What is six to the power of minus one? (p16)

17 What are the missing words? (p17)

To multiply powers of the same number you _____ the indices.

To divide powers of the same number you _____ the indices.

To take the power of a power you _____ the indices.

18 Work out **a** $(6 \times 10^5) \times (2 \times 10^4)$ **b** $(2.5 \times 10^5) + (3.4 \times 10^4)$. (pp19–20)

19 What does the standard form button look like on your calculator? (p20)

20 What does BIDMAS stand for? Work out $5^2 - 2 \times (7 - 3)$. (p21)

21 In algebra, what is a 'term'? What is an 'expression'? (p22)

22 Work out $\frac{x}{3} + \frac{4x}{3}$. (p22)

23 Multiply out the brackets: **a** $a(4a + b)$ **b** $-3(c - d)$ **c** $(a + 3)(a - 2)$ (p23)

24 Solve $7x - 4 = 10$. (p24)

25 Given that $y = 4x^3$, work out the value of y when $x = 2$. (p25)

26 What does 'making x the subject of a formula' mean? (p26)

27 What are the first five square and triangular numbers? (p27)

28 Find the nth term of these: **a** 6, 10, 14, 18, ... **b** 2, 5, 10, 17, ... (p28)

29 Find the inverse function of $x \to 2x + 4$. (p29)

30 What should you construct before drawing a graph? (p30)

31 How do you work out the gradient of a line? (p31)

32 How do you know if the gradient is positive or negative? (p31)

33 In '$y = mx + c$', what do m and c tell you? (p31)

34 What does the graph of $y = -x$ look like? (p32)

35 What does the gradient in a distance–time graph tell you? (p33)

36 What are the four inequality symbols, and what do they mean? (p34)

37 When showing inequalities on a number line, what do ○ and ● mean? (p34)

38 When showing inequalities on a graph, what does a broken line mean? (p35)

Speedy revision test (2)

39 Why is there no excuse for getting simultaneous equations wrong? (p36)
40 What should you do first when answering a trial & improvement question? (p38)
41 Roughly how many kilometres are there in a mile? (p39)
42 What do the angles on a straight line add up to? Angles at a point? (p40)
43 Draw diagrams to show **a** vertically opposite angles **b** alternate angles
   c corresponding angles. (p40)
44 What do the angles in a triangle add up to? What about a quadrilateral? (p41)
45 What are the two formulae concerning interior and exterior angles? (p41)
46 What is special about a *regular* polygon? (p41)
47 If a shape can be folded so that one half fits exactly on the other, what is it
   said to have? (p42)
48 What is the order of rotation symmetry of a square? (p42)
49 Fill in the blanks.
   A translation is defined by a _____ and _____. (p43)
   A rotation is described by its _____and an _____ _____. (p44)
   To describe an enlargement you give its _____ and ____ ____. (p45)
50 What should you do first when working out the perimeter of a shape? (p46)
51 What is the formula for the circumference of a circle? What is π? (p46)
52 Give the formulae for the area of a triangle, rectangle, parallelogram, trapezium
   and circle. (pp47–48)
53 What are the formulae for the arc length and sector area of a circle? (p49)
54 What are the two circle theorems you should know? (p49)
55 What is Pythagoras' theorem? (p50)
56 What are the formulae for sin, cos and tan? (p52)
57 Give the formulae for the volume of a cuboid, prism and cylinder. (p54)
58 The lengths in a shape are enlarged by a scale factor *k*. What happens to the
   area? What happens to the volume? (p58)
59 What are the four conditions for congruent triangles? (p58)
60 What are the three things you should know about bearings? (p59)
61 Sketch the formula triangles for speed and density. (p60)
62 What are the four loci that you should know? Draw accurate diagrams. (p62)
63 How do you work out the mean, median, mode and range? (p63)
64 What is discrete data? What is continuous data? (p64)
65 Which group does 20 belong to: $10 \leqslant n < 20$ or $20 \leqslant n < 30$? (p66)
66 Joining the middle of the tops of the bars in a frequency diagram gives what? (p66)
67 How do you estimate the mean from a grouped frequency table? (p67)
68 What is the group with the highest frequency called? (p67)
69 What is a line graph good at showing? (p68)
70 Sketch a scatter graph that shows negative correlation. (p69)
71 How do you work out the interquartile range? (p71)
72 What is the formula used to work out theoretical probability? (p72)
73 If A and B are mutually exclusive what are P(Not A) and P(A or B)? (p72)
74 What is the formula used to work out experimental probability? (p73)
75 If A and B are independent events, what is P(A and B)? (p73)

TEST answers

Page 4 Multiples, factors & prime factors
1 **a** 5, 10, 15, 20, 25 **b** 8, 16, 24, 32, 40
   c 6, 12, 18, 24, 30 **d** 9, 18, 27, 36, 45
2 **a** 1, 2, 4, 8 **b** 1, 2, 4, 8, 16, 32
   c 1, 2, 4, 5, 8, 10, 20, 40
3 **a** $2 \times 2 \times 3 \times 3 = 2^2 \times 3^2$
   b $2 \times 2 \times 3 \times 7 = 2^2 \times 3 \times 7$

Page 5 LCM & HCF
1 **a** $2 \times 2 \times 2 \times 2 \times 3 \times 3 = 144$
   b $2 \times 5 \times 5 \times 19 = 950$
2 **a** $2 \times 2 \times 3 = 12$ **b** $2 \times 2 = 4$
3 LCM $= 2 \times 2 \times 2 \times 3 \times 7 = 168$, HCF $= 2$

Page 7 Rounding (2)
1 27 900, 2900, 100 **2** 0.58, 0.02, 12.88
3 350, 1.0, 0.81 **4** **a** 5 **b** 1000

Page 8 Fractions (1)
1 $\frac{5}{8}$ **2** **a** $\frac{2}{3}$ **b** $\frac{3}{4}$ **c** $\frac{2}{5}$
3 **a** $\frac{8}{9}$ **b** $\frac{1}{8}$
4 $\frac{5}{3}$ **5** $3\frac{1}{3}$

Page 9 Fractions (2)
1 **a** $\frac{10}{49}$ **b** $\frac{2}{3}$ **c** $\frac{1}{3}$ **d** $\frac{9}{14}$ **e** £22

Page 11 Percentages (2)
1 **a** 37.5 g **b** 212.5 g **2** £20
3 Price without VAT is £80 **4** 12.5%

Page 12 Fractions, decimals & percentages (1)
1 **a** $\frac{11}{100}$ **b** $\frac{5}{100} = \frac{1}{20}$ **c** $\frac{6}{10} = \frac{3}{5}$ **d** $\frac{15}{100} = \frac{3}{20}$
2 **a** 0.7 **b** 70% **3** $\frac{35}{100} = \frac{7}{20}$

Page 13 Fractions, decimals & percentages (2)
145%, 3.45, $4\frac{1}{8}$, 4.2

Page 14 Ratio & proportion (2)
1 **a** 1 : 6 **b** 9 : 5 **c** 350 : 3
2 240 ml : 560 ml **3** £6.75

Page 15 Negative numbers
a –4 **b** 30 **c** –144 **d** –3 **e** –26 **f** 20

Page 17 Powers & roots (2)
1 **a** 144 **b** 64 **c** 32 **d** 1 **e** 100 **f** $\frac{1}{100} = 0.01$
2 **a** 6 **b** 8 **c** 10 **d** 3 **3** **a** 7^7 **b** 2^5 **c** 5^{24}

Page 18 Standard index form (1)
a 3.45×10^2 **b** 2.4×10^{-4} **c** 4.5×10^4
d 7.64×10^8 **e** 2.453×10^{-6} **f** 1.0×10^7

Page 19 Standard index form (2)
a 3700 **b** 0.000 44 **c** 5 430 000 **d** 0.000 001 2

Page 20 Standard index form (3)
1 **a** 2×10^{10} **b** 8.2×10^7 **c** 2×10^3 **d** 2×10
   e 2.4×10^5 **f** 7.64×10^4 **g** 4×10^{-3} **h** 8.13×10^7

Page 21 Calculations with brackets
a 7 **b** 36.4 **c** 7 **d** 2

Page 22 Using letters
1 **a** $3t$ **b** $4n$ **c** $3y$ **d** $4x + 2$ **2** **a** $\frac{6x}{5}$ **b** $\frac{3}{d}$

Page 23 Brackets
a $4x + 8$ **b** $mn + 7m$ **c** $a^2 + ab$ **d** $-4d + 20$
e $x^2 + 5x + 6$ **f** $x^2 - 3x - 10$ **g** $x^2 + 2x + 1$

Page 24 Equations
1 **a** $x = 3$ **b** $x = 8$
2 **❶** $x = 4$ **❷** $x = 2$ **a** $x = 2$ **b** $x = 2$

Page 25 Formulae & substitution
1 $C = 25h$ **2** £200 **3** **a** $a = 11$ **b** $a = 19$

Page 26 Rearranging formulae
1 **a** $q = \frac{\sqrt{p}}{2}$ **b** $q = \frac{\sqrt{p}}{9}$
2 **a** $a = 1 - 3b$ **b** $a = 2b$

Page 27 Sequences & number patterns (1)
1 **a** 17 **b** 48 **c** 5 **2** 14 **3** **a** 7 **b** 105 **c** 205

Page 28 Sequences & number patterns (2)
a $3n + 4$ **b** $4n - 3$ **c** $n^2 + 3$

Page 29 Functions & mappings
1 **a** 22 **b** 2 **c** $x \rightarrow 5x + 2$
2 **a** $x \rightarrow 10 - x$
   b The function and its inverse are the same.

Page 30 Straight-line graphs (1)
a

x	–2	–1	0	1	2
$y = 3x + 2$	–4	–1	2	5	8

b
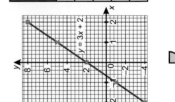

Page 31 Straight-line graphs (2)
$y = 5x + 4$

Page 32 Graphs you should know
a, b
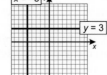
c–h See page 32.

TEST answers

Page 33 Real-life graphs
1 The train starts at station A and travels to station C at a constant speed. The train waits at station C before travelling to station B. The train waits at station B and then travels more slowly back to station A.

2 5

Page 35 Inequalities (2)
1 a −4, −3, −2, −1, 0, 1

b

2 a $x < 2$

b

3

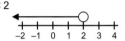

4 a $y \leqslant 2$

b
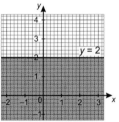

Page 36 Simultaneous equations (1)
1 $x = 4, y = 1$ 2 $x = 1, y = -1$

3 Their graphs are parallel, so they do not cross.

Page 37 Simultaneous equations (2)
1 $x = 5, y = 4$ 2 $x = -2, y = 2$

Page 38 Trial & improvement
1 $x = 3.77$ 2 2.3

Page 39 Units of measurement & accuracy
a 13.5 kg, 14.5 kg   b 2.95 cm, 3.05 cm

Page 40 Angles & parallel lines
$a = 65°, b = 56°, c = d = 124°, e = 38°, f = 128°$

Page 41 Polygons
1 49°

2 a Interior = 90°, exterior = 90°

b Interior = 120°, exterior = 60°

Page 42 Symmetry
a i 2 ii 2 b i 1 ii 1 c i 3 ii 3

Q & A Other examples include:

Page 44 Transformations (2)
1 a Translation $\begin{bmatrix} -7 \\ 2 \end{bmatrix}$

b Reflection in the line $y = x$

c Rotation of 270° about (1, 0)

2
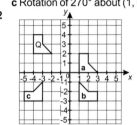

Page 45 Transformations (3)
1
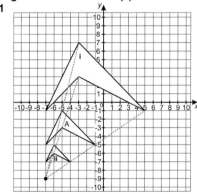

2 a Enlargement with centre (−1, 1), s.f. $\frac{1}{2}$

b Enlargement with centre (7, −3), s.f. 2

Page 46 Perimeter & circumference
1 a 28 cm b 28 cm

2 50.24 cm (using $\pi = 3.14$)

Page 47 Areas of triangles & quadrilaterals
a 42 cm² b 33 cm² c 18 cm² d 27 m²

Page 48 Areas of circles & composite shapes
a 153.86 cm² (using $\pi = 3.14$) b 122.5 cm²

Page 49 More circles
a 6.28 cm to 2 d.p. b 9.42 cm² to 2 d.p.

TEST answers

Page 51 Pythagoras' theorem (2)
1 a 12.5 cm **b** 12.1 cm **c** 19.6 km
2 a 10.6 units **b** 19.2 units
3 a (7.5, 9) **b** (18, 3.5)

Page 53 Trigonometry (2)
1 a 31.0° (tan) **b** 7.5 cm (cos)
     c 13 cm (sin)
2 19.6 m (tan)

Page 55 Volume & surface area (2)
1 a 600 m³, 660 m² **b** 126 m³, 152.4 m²
     c 2261.9 cm³, 980.2 cm² (curved surface is
     a rectangle, width same as circumference)
2 a 6 × 10⁸ cm³, 6.6 × 10⁶ cm²
     c 0.002 261 9 m³, 0.098 02 m²

Page 56 Dimensions
a Area **b** None (volume + number) **c** Area
d None (π is a number) **e** Length **f** Volume

Page 57 Congruent & similar shapes (1)
1 a Congruent **b** Neither **2** x = 8 (s.f. is 2)

Page 58 Congruent & similar shapes (2)
1 a 1 : 16 **b** 1 : 64 **2** See page 58.

Page 59 Bearings & scale drawings
1 a 090° **b** 270° **2** 100 km

Page 60 Compound measures
1 40 minutes **2** 1000 kg

Page 62 Constructions & loci (2)
3

Ends should
be semicircles

Page 63 Mean, median, mode, range (1)
Mode = 4, median = 5, mean = 6, range = 8

Page 64 Discrete & continous data
a Continuous **b** Discrete

Page 65 Collecting data & two-way tables
1 There is no option for 1 dog.
2

	Black	Red	Blue	Total
Boys own	14	**1**	11	26
Girls own	7	7	**20**	34
Total	21	8	31	60

Page 66 Frequency tables (1)
1

Number, n	Tally	Frequency
0 ≤ n < 10	|||	3
10 ≤ n < 20	|||	3
20 ≤ n < 30	|||	3
30 ≤ n < 40	⧗⧗	5
40 ≤ n < 50	||	2
	Total	16

2 a

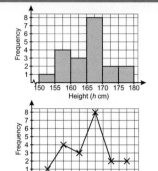

b

Page 67 Frequency tables (2)
a

Height (h cm)	Tally	Frequency
150 ≤ h < 155			1
155 ≤ h < 160	||||	4
160 ≤ h < 165	|||	3
165 ≤ h < 170	⧗⧗ |||	8
170 ≤ h < 175	||	2
175 ≤ h < 180	||	2

b 3310 ÷ 20 = 165.5 cm (midpoints: 152.5, etc)
c 165 ≤ h < 170 **d** 165 ≤ h < 170

Page 68 Stem & leaf diagrams; line graphs
1

4	2 8 9
5	0 1 4 6 7 8 8 9
6	0 2 2 2 2 3 3 5 7 8 9 9
7	0 0 2 2 3 4 5

Key: 1 | 8 means 18

2 The number of students being late falls as
each week goes along, but more students
were late in the second week.

Page 69 Scatter graphs

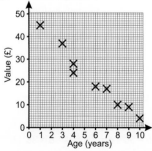

The graph shows strong negative correlation,
i.e. value decreases as age increases.

Speedy Revision

TEST answers

Page 71 Cumulative frequency (2)

TV price (£P)	Frequency	Cumulative freq.
150–	3	3
200–	8	11
250–	12	23
300–	6	29
350–	1	30

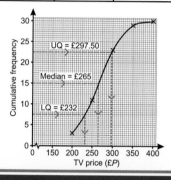

Median = £265, LQ = £232, UQ = £297.50
Interquartile range = £297.50 − £232 = £65.50

Page 73 Probability (2)

1

	First dice					
	1	2	3	4	5	6
1	1	2	3	4	5	6
2	2	4	6	8	10	12
3	3	6	9	12	15	18
4	4	8	12	16	20	24
5	5	10	15	20	25	30
6	6	12	18	24	30	36

(Second dice — left column label)

Probability of an even number $= \frac{27}{36} = \frac{3}{4}$

2 **a** $\frac{13}{52} = \frac{1}{4}$ **b** $1 - \frac{1}{13} = \frac{12}{13}$

   c $\frac{26}{52} + \frac{1}{52} = \frac{27}{52}$

3 $\frac{1}{6} \times \frac{1}{6} = \frac{1}{36}$

Index

accuracy 39
acute angles 40
addition 8, 15, 20–22, 27
adjacent 52–53
algebraic fractions 22
alternate angles 40
angles of elevation & depression 53
angles 40–41, 44, 52–53
arc length 49
area 47–49, 55–56, 58
averages 63–64, 67

bearings 59
BIDMAS 21
bisect 49, 61–62
brackets 21, 23–24

calculators 9, 15, 17, 20–21, 46, 48–49, 51–53
capacity 39
centilitre 39
centimetre 39
changing units 55
circle theorems 49

circles 46, 48–49
circumference 46
collecting data 65
collecting like terms 22
compasses 61–62
compound measures 60
congruent shapes 57–58
constructions 61–62
continuous data 64, 66
correlation 69
corresponding angles 40
cosine (cos) 52–53
cross-section 54
cube root 16
cubic graphs 32
cuboid 54–55
cumulative frequency 70–71
cylinder 54

data collection sheet 65
decimal places 6
decimals 6–7, 12–13, 18
decrease 10
denominator 8–9, 12, 17

Index

density 60
diameter 46, 48
dimensions 56
discrete data 64
distance–time graphs 33
division 9, 14–15, 17, 19, 21, 27

enlargements 45, 57
equations 24, 30–32, 34, 36–38
equilateral triangles 42, 61
equivalent fractions 8
experimental probability 73
expressions 22–25, 27
exterior angles 41

faces 55
factors 4–5
foot 39
formula triangle 60
formulae 25–26
fractions 8–9, 12–13, 17, 22
frequency diagrams 66
frequency polygons 66
frequency tables 66–67, 70
functions 29

gallon 39
gradient 31, 33
gram 39
graphs 30–33, 35–36, 68–71

highest common factor (HCF) 5, 8
hypotenuse 50–53, 58

image 43, 45
imperial units 39
improper fractions 8
inch 39
increase 10
independent events 73
indices 16–17, 21
inequalities 34–35
input 29
interior angles 41
interquartile range 71
inverse function 29

kilogram 39
kilometre 39

least common multiple (LCM) 5
line graphs 68
line of best fit 69
line symmetry 42
linear sequence 28
litre 39
loci 62
lower quartile 71

mappings 29
mass 39, 60
mean 63–64, 67
median 63–64, 67, 71
metre 39
metric units 39
midpoint 51, 66–67
mile 39
millilitre 39
millimetre 39
mirror line 43
mixed numbers 8
modal group 67
mode 63–64
multiples 4–5
multiplication 9, 15, 17, 19, 21, 23, 27
mutually exclusive 72

nearest ten, hundred or thousand 6
negative gradient 31
negative numbers 15
negative powers 16
nth term 27–28
number line 15, 34, 38
number patterns 27–28
numerator 8–9, 12

object 43
obtuse angles 40
order of operations 21
order of rotation 42
ordering 13
ounce 39
output 29

Speedy Revision